The Realities of Classroom Testing and Grading

A Guide to Performance Issues

QUENTIN DURHAM

ROWMAN & LITTLEFIELD EDUCATION
Lanham, Maryland • Toronto • Oxford
2006

Published in the United States of America
by Rowman & Littlefield Education
A Division of Rowman & Littlefield Publishers, Inc.
A wholly owned subsidiary of The Rowman & Littlefield Publishing Group, Inc.
4501 Forbes Boulevard, Suite 200, Lanham, Maryland 20706
www.rowmaneducation.com

PO Box 317
Oxford
OX2 9RU, UK

Copyright © 2006 by Quentin Durham

All rights reserved. No part of this publication may be reproduced, stored in a retrieval system, or transmitted in any form or by any means, electronic, mechanical, photocopying, recording, or otherwise, without the prior permission of the publisher.

British Library Cataloguing in Publication Information Available

Library of Congress Cataloging-in-Publication Data

Durham, Quentin, 1931–
  The realities of classroom testing and grading : a guide to performance issues / Quentin Durham.
    p. cm.
  ISBN-13: 978-1-57886-388-4 (hardcover : alk. paper)
  ISBN-10: 1-57886-388-0 (hardcover : alk. paper)
  ISBN-13: 978-1-57886-389-1 (pbk. : alk. paper)
  ISBN-10: 1-57886-389-9 (pbk. : alk. paper)
  1. Educational tests and measurements. 2. Grading and marking (Students) I. Title.
  LB3051.D677 2006
  371.27—dc22   2005032400

∞™ The paper used in this publication meets the minimum requirements of American National Standard for Information Sciences—Permanence of Paper for Printed Library Materials, ANSI/NISO Z39.48-1992.
Manufactured in the United States of America.

Contents

Introduction		1
1	Why Bother to Test?	5
2	Subjectivity	17
3	Relevance	23
4	Validity	31
5	Design	47
6	Open-Book Exams	57
7	Performance Exams	65
8	Forced-Answer Exams	71
9	Essay Exams	81
10	Grading	93
11	Posttest Activities	103

Introduction

The primary function of schools is the education of students. Any activity not leading to that end should be eliminated.

Students are never graded on what they know. What they actually know never counts. Both school and life punish and reward based on what some observer—parent, employer, college pooh-bah, rich uncle—perceives the students to know. In schools, that "some person" is almost always the teacher.

For the first few years of their careers, at least, teachers tend to teach and evaluate as they were taught and evaluated. They decide when it is time for an exam, decide the content and format of the exam, administer it to a cheering throng of students, evaluate student responses, establish some sort of grading system that offends everybody equally, record the grades someplace, and eventually get back to teaching.

There are numerous variations possible. In the earliest grades, for example, almost all instruction, assessment, and reporting are done nose-to-nose with the individual kids, and teachers rarely feel much need for gradebook-centered grading systems. Facing the same group of kids all day long, the teacher quickly acquires a mental database of vastly more student information than could be found in any gradebook—strengths, weaknesses, favorite pets, detested siblings, unacceptable vegetables, and so on. Parent conferences often replace written reports, and the teacher simply relies on her memory and experience to provide the parents and kids with a sound and useful estimate of student performance.

At about the junior high level, as often is the case in connection with adolescents, things become more complex. With more students and several classes, the teacher is less familiar with the individual student's performance, and gradebook-amenable pencil-and-paper exams are increasingly relied on to help assure that credit is given where credit is due.

At the university level, few students have any meaningful, nose-to-nose contact with the professor. The teacher is almost completely detached from student performance, student understanding is generally assessed solely by written exams, and the gradebook reigns supreme.

Usually safe, reasonably comfortable, and occasionally effective, it is not surprising that classroom assessment and reporting methods tend to be self-perpetuating. Unfortunately, many of the techniques and procedures that have been passed along as gospel for generations may be in serious need of review and adjustment.

With luck and as experience is acquired, classroom trench-warfare reality eventually sets in. What worked more or less okay 'way back then may not be appropriate today. Furthermore, with experience, teachers increasingly see student evaluation as difficult, always necessary, generally useful, rarely entertaining, and only one part of the much larger educational process. They have far better things to do with their time than fool around with evaluative niceties. They almost never have hundreds of tidy bell-shaped students upon whom to base tidy bell-shaped grade curves. Few have much enthusiasm for "product-moment coefficients of correlation" charts or Kuder-Richardson formulae.

The intent of *Classroom Testing and Grading* is to use common English, common sense, and perhaps a touch of humor to explore and illuminate such fundamental classroom concerns as

What is accomplished by testing and grading?

What characteristics are shared by all test types?

What characteristics are unique to specific test types?

What is the best way to report student efforts?

What can be accomplished during postexam activities?

It is hoped that *Classroom Testing and Grading*'s treatment of these topics will both answer some questions and provide a starting point for further discussion and pedagogical harangues—no screaming, please.

A couple of points probably need emphasis. In this book, the word "classroom" is broadly defined to be anyplace from which a student knows more exiting than entering—single-teacher classrooms, woodshops, senior proms, concert halls, corporate training facilities, and jails. By this definition, the cockpit of a supersonic aircraft is a classroom—most assuredly the most expensive classroom ever.

As teacher-generated exams are the lifeblood of all education, this book includes little discussion of standardized exams—SATs and their ilk. While these exams are the focus of today's newspaper headlines and much administrative anxiety, they have little useful effect on the typical student's education compared to the day-to-day exams written by the classroom teacher, and they are beyond the scope of this book.

Because its intention is to provide practical testing and grading assistance to teachers, students, and parents, this book is often, perhaps most of the time, in variance with common EdBiz vocabulary. An ongoing effort has been made to avoid the jargon and blather that too often make educational literature unapproachable and function-free.

1

Why Bother to Test?

The primary function of all classroom activities is to assist in the student's education, and teacher-generated exams are a major part of this process.

TEACHER'S EVALUATION AND REVIEW
Undoubtedly the most useful result of any testing effort is to provide the student and parents with the teacher's timely and experienced evaluation of the kid's performance: to have his work intelligently observed, analyzed, corrected, and clearly reported. And of course it is also useful to make suggestions regarding the avoidance of future disasters. How these worthwhile goals are accomplished varies widely among students, teachers, and test types.

With performance courses, the teacher's assessment is made while the student actually demonstrates how much he or she knows about what has been taught. The music teacher listens to Alphonse assault a defenseless violin or give the three-string guitar the old what-for. The English teacher evaluates the student's ability to deliver a semi-intelligible oral report, and the kindergarten teacher watches a small mathematician explore the notion that two Oreos and two chocolate-chip cookies add up to four good things. This assessment technique—all tidily direct and with few irrelevant distractions—is about as good as one person's assessment of another's understanding can be.

Teacher assessment and reporting of student performance on indirect exams is far less useful to the student than that provided by performance exams. Essay exam evaluations, for example, are done by the teacher at her solitary leisure, often in the middle of the night, and rarely nose-to-nose with the student. Eventually the student gets his paper back with a depressing number of red markings thereupon, and that is *that*. Any additional, more personal assessment generally will have to wait for the review process—an iffy proposition at best.

Teachers' reporting methods vary. While the basketball coach may be quite at ease screaming his evaluations from the sideline, the kindergarten teacher probably selects a less stridently enthusiastic reporting style. In any case, and while the student may not agree with the teacher's assessment ("Life's full of green bananas, Tarzan!"), the point is to make the teacher's assessment of the student's strengths, weaknesses, and future possibilities as clear and useful as possible.

STUDY GOADS

Upcoming Exams

Whatever their formats, tests are very effective study goads. Facing the certainty of an algebra test in the next few days, many students are sincerely motivated to buy the appropriate textbook and try to relate it to whatever the teacher has been yapping about recently.

Bank Accounts

Many students (and their doting parents) consider grades to be something of a bank account—a bank account that they hope can be used to "purchase" the goodies that school success promises. Enrollment in future classes, for example, often depends on adequate grades in current classes. One is not allowed to take calculus without decent algebra grades, and entrance to the College of One's Choice is controlled to a large extent by success in high school evaluations. Naval pilots are simply not allowed to attempt to land on a carrier's deck until they have demonstrated the ability to land successfully on a dirt airstrip far away from any property more valuable than the occasional cow.

Fun

A surprising characteristic of many exams is that, under some conditions and with some students, they are both fun to take and fun to study for.

"What? What complete nonsense! All exams are vile and distasteful!"

Well—consider. The only proper exam for a high school quarterback is to ask the student to play the game—right out there in front of everybody—and assess his performance. This may be a highly anxiety-producing event, but it is also fun. Similarly, a three-minute kettledrum solo not only provides the teacher with a chance to evaluate the three-foot-two-inch soloist's performance and ability to see over the top of the thing, it also is entertaining to the kid—she has the stage, everybody is listening, she knows what she is doing, and she knows it is coming out well . . . "Golly, this *is* a kick!" THUMPA-WHACKA-BOOM!

And of course there is no point in downplaying the entertainment value some students find in comparing their grades with those of their colleagues. "Ha ha! Suzy got a D- while I got a straight D! Ha Ha!" And within certain hormonal groups, the entertainment aspects related to the use of the family car are often tied to school progress as witnessed by grades, progress reports, and report cards.

Curiosity

One of the better study goads is simple curiosity; the student finds herself interested in the material the teacher has been presenting and elects to follow up on it. The basketball student may take a certain delight in shooting baskets all Saturday afternoon, and she probably would take exception to the notion that she was studying. Same thing with the history student who stumbles onto the astonishing realization that he finds the third-century reign of Queen Uurrlnf The Unpronounceable interesting and enjoys reading about (i.e., studying) this justifiably obscure character.

Peer Review

In most performance classes, the student knows for certain that his efforts will be viewed both by the teacher and his classmates, and this certainty can encourage the student to study with determination, enthusiasm, and zeal. A typical scenario has the student muttering to himself:

> Man, I can just see the whole class sitting there listening to my speech. Dead silence at first, then smiling, then giggling. Then somebody starts laughing and hooting and foot stomping. With me standing there sweating... Maybe I'd better go over it just one more time.

LEARNING EXPERIENCES

"'Aha!' Phenomenon"

A surprisingly useful function of most testing formats is the "'Aha!' phenomenon." This is the common event in which a student, in the process of taking an exam, is taught something by the exam itself. Plowing through a few dozen multiple-choice questions, for example, the student unexpectedly stumbles across some bit of information that had totally escaped him until then:

> Okay, okay. The right answer has to be one of these four. Gotta be. But I don't... Wait a minute. Wait...

Then slapping his forehead with his hand he exclaims

Aha! So that's how it works!

Viewing Peer Performance

"Oh! I see. One blows into *that* end of the trombone. Fascinating!"

An often underrated student benefit of testing is exposure to peer performances. While this doesn't happen much with indirect exams, it is a common feature of performance classes such as art and music.

Typically, the school orchestra violinists are acutely aware of, and may actually benefit from, a nearby trumpeter's blastissimo sins of commission. It is difficult for a baseball batter to remain unaware of the opposing pitcher's expertise and technique as the latest in a long, uninterrupted sequence of strike balls whizzes by in what promises to be a depressing game. And a skydiver, while visiting a colleague recuperating in the hospital, may pause to consider what lessons there are to be learned from his friend's memorable performance.

Additionally, it may be worthwhile to note that many of the most important classroom lessons are unrelated to anybody's curriculum; they are neither planned nor graded but are the result of watching one's classroom colleagues perform. A short soap opera may serve to illustrate:

Tim was a clever and highly likeable young man who had struggled with cerebral palsy all his life. As a member of a history class taught by a teacher who shall remain unnamed but never forgotten, he was expected to deliver an oral report of the sort demanded of high school seniors. His topic was the Sacramento River or something equally enthralling. And there he stood—sweat running down his beet-red face, drooling onto his shirt, scattering his carefully prepared notes all over the floor, and blathering on incomprehensibly. Some of his classmates stared at the ceiling. Some stared at the floor. Some stared out into space. Some stared at their shoes. All would have done anything to have been anywhere—*anywhere*—other than in that classroom watching their friend's pathetic efforts.

Then the teacher interrupted. "That's okay, Tim, I'll finish."

Heads snapped up. Jaws dropped open. "How can that idiot teacher be so stupidly insensitive not to see what's important here? Forget the miserable Sacramento River. TIM IS GIVING AN ORAL REPORT!"

No curriculum. No testing. No grading. Just sudden, hard-edged, lifelong learning. The best.

Rite of Passage

For both students and teachers, evaluation efforts can serve as a summation, a rite of passage, and a time, perhaps, to consider what potential disasters loom on the horizon.

Teacher to self,

> Thank goodness that miserable topic is behind us. I hate it and the kids hate it. I wonder if I'll ever understand it well enough to like it. Probably not. Onward!

Or perhaps

> Finally! So much for *Charlotte's Web*. Look out, *Winnie the Pooh*, here we come!

Furthermore, and whatever the exam format, test-writing sessions themselves can provide the teacher with a chance for the reflection and overview that

- Encourages planning. "What do I want the students to get out of this part of the course?"
- Encourages review of past tests and other history. "Let's see. What, if anything, did we do since the last exam? Guess maybe the thing to do is go back and review earlier exams."
- Encourages review of evaluation procedures and methods. "How can I best evaluate the students' understanding and performance? What format should I use? Same as last time?"
- Encourages thoughtful anticipation of probable answers. "What sorts of answers can I expect, and which will I accept?"

Viewing Student Success

One of the reasons why many otherwise rational people remain in teaching is the pleasure they derive from watching their students' successes. The kindergarten teacher sees a child finally master the graphic complexities of the letter W ... The skiing instructor watches her student actually arrive at the bottom of the slope without any assistance from stretcher-bearing paramedics or helicopters ...

Control

At least one test function is counterproductive: the use of the testing/grading process as a classroom control technique. Says the teacher,

> If you don't quiet down and pay attention, you're going to get an exam that will curdle your hair!

While this is generally considered dismal teaching technique, it is an easy trap for the harried teacher, and there is no denying that it happens. Announcing an upcoming exam is one thing. Using it as a threat is another.

PARENTAL INVOLVEMENT

Most studies indicate that the primary predictor of student academic success is parental involvement; all else being equal, the students blessed with lots of parental involvement get the better grades. However, parents can only provide this vital function if they have up-to-date access to their child's performance. This necessary information can come from several sources—some better than others.

1. Asking the kid

Many parents keep up to date via the simple gambit of asking the student, "How is school these days, Alphonse?" Depending on the student, the class, and other variables, there always is some measure of "editorializing" between student vision and academic reality. Nevertheless, the parents' obvious concern in itself can have a significant effect on student performance. The kid knows that the parents either know what's going on, or sooner or later are going to find out. Knowing whatever happens in the classroom will probably have repercussions at home, many students feel a strong urge to see that the news going home is as good as possible—even if it means increased study efforts.

2. Report cards, grades, and other formalized teacher evaluations

The most common, and surprisingly effective, way to encourage parental involvement is to provide the parent with timely, frequent, and complete progress information. A weekly report card, perhaps? Kids may be less than charmed at such a suggestion, but considering the ease with which current microchippery can accomplish this, there is little excuse for teacher or parent to be satisfied by quarterly—or worse, semestral—reports.

3. Direct observation

As the student's efforts are generally accomplished out of public view, parental involvement in indirect subjects such as history and Swahili is difficult to impossible. But performance subjects such as music or PE generally have testing procedures that are amenable to, and strongly suggest, parental presence and involvement. Parents and other doting relatives can attend (and assess) a student's musical performance or a baseball game. They can quietly observe (and assess) the student play the alto strudelhorn, or simply sit in the front row of a soccer match and scream, "GO GET 'EM! KILL 'EM!" In either example, it would be foolish to suggest that the student's performance is unaffected by the knowledge that a number of her highly critical, birthday-present-giving relatives are in the audience.

Whatever the format, the assessments made by parents alone may be somewhat less than perfect. The parents may be unaware of appropriate performance standards for students of his age and background. What constitutes good, bad, or indifferent trombone performance depends on many factors, most certainly including the student's age, experience, and general wit. Also, the student's parents are likely to have probably-justified biases regarding the student's behavior—anytime, anyplace, in school and elsewhere:

Jeez! Can't that kid ever do anything: (Check one)

❏ right?
❏ wrong?

4. Parent/teacher conferences
Many teacher-parent interactions are accomplished not on the phone or in a cozy conference room after school, but nose-to-nose during such wondrous civic events as Back-to-School Night. While these contacts generally have only limited utility as the time is short and the line is long, on occasion a vast amount of information is exchanged very quickly:

Teacher: Good to see you, Mr. and Mrs. Sackbutt. Your son has explained how your untimely deaths have prevented him from devoting as much time to his schoolwork as he'd like. Are you both feeling better now?

Or

Parent (hand extended, teeth exposed): How come my adorable daughter gets the same crummy grade in English all the time? Haven't you teachers learned *nothing* in the four years she's been in third grade?

Many responses come to the experienced teacher's mind, but common sense usually prevails.

BENEFITS (IF ANY) TO OTHERS FROM STUDENT EVALUATION
While the board, the administration, and some other groups may fuss about teacher-generated exams and their manipulation, they generally choose not to get involved in such day-to-day classroom concerns but

instead to zero in on the standardized exams that often inspire newspaper headlines, administrative hysteria, and school board dither. Considering the alternative, that's probably okay.

Administration

The administration's interest in classroom evaluation and grading is fleeting at best, only surfacing when there seems to be a problem. And the problem along these lines most likely to cause administrative upset is the teacher who hands out more lousy grades than the administration thinks is good for appearances. Too many Fs on too many report cards are almost certain to inspire immediate and enthusiastic administrative palpitations and angst. On the other hand, too many As simply don't present a problem:

> Principal: My, what a wonderful teacher Ms. Hardscrabble is! Just look at all those wonderful grades! Every one of her thousands of pupils earned an A. We haven't had a single parental complaint in the 68.7 years she has been on our staff—teaching whatever it is she teaches.

School Board

For good reasons, today's school boards fixate almost exclusively on standardized exams and the effort required to assure that this year's scores look better than last year's. Teacher-designed evaluation procedures are usually considered part of that soggy quagmire of things the administration is supposed to take care of or make go away. And that may be okay; classroom evaluation is probably well served by that arrangement. Any meddling in a teacher's evaluation struggles by the school board—or anybody else, for that matter—is unlikely to improve, ease, or facilitate an already difficult process.

College Entry Pooh-Bahs

While it may only be because college exams ask the same fool questions as high school exams, it is generally conceded that high school grades are fine predictors of college success, and many colleges accept and reject incoming students at least partially on the basis of high school grades. This is not, unfortunately, the trend. Standardized exams today often have greater impact on college entry pooh-bahs than do high school evaluations. While the actual size of this impact depends on the college, the pooh-bah, and whatever other entrance criteria the college's regents currently find attractive, college-bound students are well-advised to do everything necessary to get as good standardized test scores as possible even though these tests and resulting scores have essentially no useful connection with high school curricula, grades, learning, or (as has often been suggested) life.

Employers

Only a very few employers ever ask, or have the legal right to ask, to see a potential employee's transcript—the military and some professional boards being possible exceptions. Many employers assume (with some justification) that after being recently evicted from one academic program or another—kindergarten through graduate school—the applicant remains totally ignorant of anything useful, and no matter how much his third-grade teacher admired his penmanship, the klutz will have to be trained from scratch just like all the others.

2
Subjectivity

Subjective: Conditions viewed through the medium of one's own mind or individuality.
Objective: Free from personal prejudices, feelings, or opinions.

Much of the testing literature is so full of blather and gas regarding subjectivity (bad) and objectivity (good), one could easily be led to believe that there are two kinds of evaluative processes. There are not. Extensively footnoted, career-enhancing nonsense aside, a fundamental reality of all evaluative methods—personal, business, academic, and probably Pearly Gates—is that they are all completely, ultimately, and quite properly subjective. Subjective evaluation is not only certain, it is the only rational and meaningful way one mortal can evaluate another. The question is not *whether* a particular question, test, or testing program is subjective, but rather *where* subjectivity enters the evaluative process.

As this is not exactly a concept that all authorities will support with unchecked enthusiasm, some expansion may be useful. There are two compelling reasons why all testing is ultimately subjective. The first and most painfully obvious is that in the absence of exams chiseled into stone tablets by the Great Test-Maker in the Sky, they are all written, evaluated, and otherwise manipulated, from start to finish, by people.

All evaluative systems, most assuredly including school-type exams, are the end result of a long series of choices and decisions made by highly nonobjective, error-prone, human-type people. Every step along the route, from deciding to have an exam to the final bookkeeping, involves a series of choices—choices that often as not are resolved by reference to personal biases, past experiences, old exams, old colleagues, and chicken entrails.

On performance or indirect exams, the teacher is required to make many subjective decisions. She has to select the exercises to be performed and assess the resulting student performance. If the course is English composition, the students know that they are going to be asked to compose in English, but the teacher still selects the specific topic and, eventually, grades the students' efforts. The physics student knows he will be asked to find the boiling point of some material, but the teacher decides what the appropriate material will be. Determining the boiling point of hydrogen, for example, may involve skills, tools, and a respect for life and limb uncommon in fourth graders.

Not only is the design and selection of the questions subjective, evaluation of student responses always requires subjective decisions. The geometry student who, for example, devises an elegant and unexpected solution to a run-of-the-mill problem, surely (and subjectively) deserves something extra. Or consider the history student who presents a well-reasoned and lucid argument that World War II was a direct result of some obscure king's disappointment with his daughter's choice of suitor.

"Hold it," one hears from the back row. "What about math exams? Huh? With all those numbers, math exams surely must be objective. Huh?" Not a chance. As with all other evaluation efforts, some person creates or chooses problems that she (subjectively) thinks appropriate:

Can't give a differential calculus problem to third graders, can we? Too hard.

Or

Can't give the problem 2 + 2 = ? to calculus students, can we? Too easy."

An exaggeration, of course, but who decides what's "too easy" or "too hard"? Who always decides what is an appropriate question and what is not? With luck, the teacher. Whether kindergarten arithmetic or graduate level magnetohydrodynamics, the teacher decides. The decision is completely subjective and one of the things all teachers are paid to do, and which good teachers do exceedingly well.

The second and less obvious reason why all evaluations are completely subjective is a result of the philosophical and mathematical certainty that the result of any calculation can be no more precise than the calculation's least precise element. One or one hundred precise numbers multiplied by an approximation will ultimately yield an approximation.

A fable may help. Once upon a time, the king wanted to know the depth of the ocean. Unable to get a useful number from any of his Realm Administrators, he rounded up the eighty-seven wisest people on Earth, had them rowed out into the middle of the ocean, and demanded that they take a good look and report back prontissimo.

"Sheesh," said the first, peering at the murky surface. "I haven't a clue. Maybe five feet."

"Gee, I don't know either, said the second. "Maybe five miles. Whatever the king wants."

And so it went; estimates ranged from six inches to 10,712 miles. Eventually all eighty-seven responses were recorded and delivered to the Realm Administration where at grotesque expense, they were added, averaged, collated, commingled, attacked with root-mean-squares, computerized, and otherwise massaged. Ultimately the king was informed that the ocean was 612.00718346 feet deep.

Now a number like 612.00718346 does not look like an estimate. A number like that appears to have real authority, real meaning, a pillar in the number community. Wrong. Despite all those juicy numbers on both sides of the decimal point, the average of any number of approximations is an approximation. Just one flea-bitten guess averaged in with a vast pile of tidily precise numbers will provide a final result that is exactly one flea-bitten guess. More to the matter at hand, just one flea-bitten subjective element in any evaluation procedure will provide a final result that is completely subjective. And all evaluation methods have an abundance of flea-bitten subjective elements.

A misunderstanding of this concept can lead to some colorful teacher behavior. Witness the harried English teacher who, at the approach of report card time, assigns numerical values to the letter grades in her gradebook, adds them up, averages them out to a dozen or so decimal places, and assigns letter grades based on these multi-digit fantasies. Then at the next available faculty meeting she proclaims, loudly and with vast smugness, the virtuous accuracy of her grades. "Just *look* at all those decimal places! How thrillingly precise!"

Pooh. Her basic technique—quick and dirty assignment of letter grades based on her competence, experience, and understanding—is faultless. However, her final results suggest a precision completely unsupported by the basic measurements— exactly as with the eighty-seven wise guys.

TIMING

While unknown administrative types generally (and subjectively) decide when externally imposed standardized exams are to be given, teachers often have great latitude in scheduling most other exams. One teacher may decide to give a killer test just prior to a vacation on the notion that the students will probably will do better on a test given before, rather than after, a week or two off. Another teacher may opt for having the exam after the vacation—hoping to get a better understanding of what, if anything, may actually remain in the students' heads over the longer term. Similarly, one teacher may want to test on Fridays, when what has allegedly been learned is still fresh, while another teacher may go for Monday tests in the highly iffy hope that an occasional student may actually do a little studying over the weekend.

With final exams, a common decision is to administer them on the last day of class. Such is reasonable, expected, provides the maximum days of teaching, and allows adequate time for what often are dismally slow marking and ranking procedures. An additional benefit, particularly at the university level, is that the time between the exam and when the students learn their grades is adequate for the professor to get out of town, thereby becoming unavailable for explanation, negotiation, review, or assassination.

Conversely, a final exam given prior to the last class meeting makes review and arbitration possible, is sound teaching technique, and can provide the teacher with student feedback that may be useful in the future.

Do whatever works. The point here is not to debate the relative virtues of hypothetical schedules, but rather to note that there are many options to choose from—subjectively, of course.

FORMAT

An important subjective decision is the exam format essay: forced-answer or direct. Obviously, course content will provide some major, hard-to-ignore clues. History classes suggest essay or multiple-choice exams. Art and music classes are probably best evaluated by direct observation, and it is hard to imagine evaluating a kindergarten kid by anything other than the most direct, stand-there-and-watch-her-do-it methods. Similarly, if the school board expects Coach Jacques to evaluate student "sportsmanship," essay and written exams are definitely not the order of the day.

Format selection should be a reasonably straightforward chore, but as long as subjective people decide, strange things happen. One *can* choose to assign an essay exam in a public speaking class or try to assess a PE student's sportsmanship by counting push-ups. One *can* pretend, as many standardized exams do, to evaluate a student's ability to write a coherent English sentence without actually asking the student to write a coherent English sentence. One *can*, but one should not. The decision to use an inappropriate format may be counterproductively silly, but it is no more or less subjective than to choose something more useful.

DISPLACED SUBJECTIVITY

"Aha!" one hears. "We don't have any problems with subjectivity because our school district only uses exams written by somebody else. Yessir, we go to great expense to get only the finest off-the-shelf exams money can buy. I mean, if them exams weren't a hunnert percent objective, they wouldn't be allowed to sell them, right?"

No sale. Displaced subjectivity remains subjectivity, and using somebody else's idea of how a course should be evaluated creates far more problems than it solves. Most assuredly written by mortals, off-the-shelf exams, including all standardized exams, are completely subjective. Furthermore, unless the teaching is based on the preselected exams, the exams are unlikely to have any useful relevance. And if the preselected exams *are* allowed to dictate the course content, the design of the curriculum will have been surrendered to the test makers—whoever they are and whatever their qualifications. Unfortunately, this seems to be the trend.

This is not to suggest that off-the-shelf worksheets and sample exams thoughtfully provided by some publishers are to be ignored. If the materials are useful, the teacher should feel free to use them—while keeping in mind that the decision to do so is completely subjective.

3

Relevance

Real-World Relevance: Does the exam measure what you want to find out?

Classroom Relevance: Does the exam measure how much the student knows of what has been taught?

A relevant test measures what the tester wants to find out. In education, what the tester usually wants to find out is how much the student understands about what has been taught. And note the operative phrase "has been taught." Relevance is independent of curricula; curricula dictate what is supposed to be taught, while relevance relates to what actually has been taught. In an ideal world, there would be little difference between the two, but things being as they generally are in the classroom, one shouldn't count on it. In reality, there are three curricula in everyday use: the board's, the student's, and the teacher's.

BOARD CURRICULUM

The first curriculum is the school board's curriculum. In contrast to common wisdom, it is simply untrue that this curriculum's sole function is to assist the administration in keeping the board informed as to what really isn't going on in the classroom anyhow.

School board members often fantasize about a world in which there is an exact match between the approved curriculum and what actually gets taught. Teachers would teach, and the students would learn and be evaluated on exactly what the board has ordained—or else! Changes in the approved curriculum would quickly be reflected in classroom activities. When members of the National Association Against Weather moan loudly enough, the board will see to it that the proposal is discussed in administrative meetings, fiddled with by numerous expensive specialists, and massaged by a variety of interested souls. Eventually the official curriculum will be adjusted to meet NAAW's concerns, and the district's science teachers will promptly alter their goals and techniques accordingly. A lovely concept, and there probably are several schools in the United States where, from time to time, this is the way it actually works.

STUDENT CURRICULUM

From the student's point of view, the only curricula that count are:

- Officially ignored
- Completely untaught
- Often hormone driven
- Light years beyond the scope of this book

These unstructured courses of study often address such eternal verities as

- In spite of the delights of story time and the mysteries of the alphabet, school is not all Oreos and milk.
- Girls are more interesting than boys—or the other way around.
- There is life after acne.
- Scholarships expire, grants are uncertain, and tenure is improbable.

Although these student concerns probably have more significance to life than most of what happens in most schools, if they have not been taught, they should not be part of any testing program.

TEACHER CURRICULUM

Happily for the sake of scholastic tranquillity, what the board says should be taught and what actually is taught when the classroom door is closed are—within the limits of common sense anyhow—often similar. By and large, what is taught in most classrooms is a fair approximation of what the board thinks is being taught. The math teacher teaches the prescribed branches of math at the appropriate level, probably using the board-approved textbook quite often. The French teacher teaches French in general alignment with what she thinks the board has in mind. And the architectural history professor—having decided that the board of regents' expressed interest in third-century drinking fountains isn't what it really wants—prattles on about Romanesque cow barns. Close enough.

CURRICULAR RELEVANCE

In a world awash with stuff students are supposed to learn, there is little question that some skills and understandings are more important than others, and that the teaching and acquisition of these skills and understandings should have absolutely top priority. But if what is being taught is history, deficiencies or abundances in untaught skills are irrelevant and should not be allowed to affect a student's history grade. Unless grammar is actively taught in a botany class, a student's understanding and proper use of grammar should have exactly the same effect on his botany grade as his understanding and proper use of dental floss. None.

To exaggerate for clarity, if a math teacher, for whatever unimaginable reasons, has been teaching the more entertaining aspects of mushroom reproduction, a relevant exam would attempt to evaluate how much the student knows about the things molds do when nobody is looking. Any questions relating to *untaught* materials—mathematical or other—are irrelevant. The teacher may be a candidate for residence in the State Home for the Permanently Befuddled, but not because of any lack of evaluative relevance.

Attributes relevant in one context often are irrelevant in another. The math teacher may decide that class participation is irrelevant in his class, while the basketball coach understandably ranks attendance high on his list of student "things to do." While accuracy may be a highly relevant quality for a physics student, the word may almost have no meaning to the painter. Speed is a relevant characteristic in a keyboarding class, but as life seldom puts much value on writing speed, it probably should be considered irrelevant in an English composition class.

Similarly, a question can be satisfyingly relevant in completely different subject areas. For example, given the assignment of writing a few dozen nifty paragraphs on the effects of kitty litter technology on the carpet industry, the history student can expect to be evaluated on her grasp of one set of criteria—numbers, people, facts, historical context—along with a display of as much logic as can be expected from history students. However, the English composition student should be evaluated on a different set of criteria—clarity of presentation, grammar, syntax, spelling, and all the other things of which English teachers approve.

The concept of relevance seems simple, but idiotic exceptions abound. At least one expensive and respected standardized exam claims to test spelling skills by asking students to find the *mis*spelled words lurking in a list. By failing to discriminate between spelling skills as taught in class and demanded in life, and the editorial skills demanded of almost nobody, the test becomes exactly, perfectly irrelevant. The official explanation of this folly is that "there is a strong correlation between success on this exam and real spelling achievement." The real reason for this nonsense, of course, is that this is the only machine-gradable exam that its vendors can call a spelling test without risking a terminal case of the giggles. A relevant spelling exam asks students to spell words—exactly as life and the teacher (Ms. Hardscrabble) do.

None of the above should suggest that an occasional, deliberately irrelevant test question is always bad. Such questions might be thought of as representing a "lateral relevance." These are questions in which the teacher's real aim is both devious and useful. For example,

- Asking transparently foolish questions to lighten things up, get the juices flowing, or reduce the incidence of dread *Testitis panicus*:

    True/True. This is the silliest exam I've ever been asked to take.

- Inserting a question that is intended not to ask something, but rather to teach something via the "'Aha!' phenomenon." The teacher exploits the students' rapt attention to assure the transmission of important but curriculum-irrelevant information:

    Please complete the following sentence:

    "The next student to spill goop all over the floor will be _____."

- Questions deliberately designed to provide the teacher with irrelevant but useful information:

    If you have recently been bitten by a cobra but are planning to take biology next year, please mark . . .

Since actually including any of these "laterally relevant" questions in the grading scheme would be nonsense—likely to encourage both parental disapproval and administrative fidgets—it is important to assure the students that while the questions serve some particular need, they will not affect anybody's grade.

All of this is nice theory. However, in the real-world, classroom variety, it is very difficult to prevent "irrelevant" skills from affecting the teacher's perception of student understanding. It is not easy for a teacher to resist downgrading a music appreciation student for despicable handwriting, or to resist punishing a history student for misplacing a modifier or allowing a whatzit to dangle, even though proper handwriting, modifiers, and whatzits have not been taught in that class. But the attempt must be made, even at the significant cost of slower, more difficult marking and longer turnaround times. The attempt is part of what many teachers are underpaid to do.

To reinforce the tenet that teaching degenerates after kindergarten, one may note that primary teachers manage, with notable success and in the absence of all indirect evaluation methods, to teach rooms full of essentially illiterate students. How? Early grade evaluation is almost exclusively direct, hands on, and performance oriented. These little kids are asked to *do* what they have learned—perhaps by consistently making the proper choice between GIRLS and BOYS rooms—even under the stress of needing to use one or the other NOW!

As it is always silly to ask illiterate *little* kids to respond to written exams, such exams are equally inappropriate for illiterate *big* kids. For all students with English difficulties, kindergartners or anybody else, direct exams are the only evaluation methods that have any possibility of significant validity. Hence the lovely "Catch-22":

- Direct exams are the only rational evaluation methods for students with English difficulties; however,
- Many courses are not amenable to direct evaluation. How tidy.

There really are only a couple of approaches to the problem of providing relevant written exams for students with inadequate English skills. The first is the common, near universal, college-level approach that raises educational silliness to new heights: ignore the problem. Assignments are made in English, tests are written in English, student responses are evaluated in English, and grades are assigned based on these evaluations. While this may be a pedagogically faultless approach if the course is Remedial English, if the course is anything else, silliness triumphs.

The other approach is strictly for the stout of heart and tenured. The easiest, most entertaining, and most effective way to enhance relevance is to eschew indirect evaluation as far as possible and rely heavily on direct performance testing. One observes and evaluates the painter painting, the public speaking student speaking publicly, and the calculus student doing whatever it is that gets taught in calculus classes. While this approach has some obvious limits (graduate-level atomic physics, for example—far too noisy) direct methods work over a far broader range of topics than is generally acknowledged. These are the methods your first-grade teacher used exclusively, and she taught you how to *read*.

4
Validity

In a perfect world, student performance on a test would accurately reflect the student's understanding of what has been taught. A lovely concept. In order to reach this pedagogical nirvana, however, two requirements must be met. The test must be both relevant and valid. As discussed earlier, a relevant exam relates closely to what has been taught. If an exam includes all of what has been taught, and only that which has been taught, the exam is relevant.

A valid exam relates closely to what is on the exam; validity is a measure of the exam's ability to separate the sheep from the goats. Test validity is damaged by anything that obscures the teacher's perception of student understanding of the materials on the exam, and while there are exceptions, validity-harming concerns are largely within the teacher's control. If the student who knows the most about the materials *on the exam* gets the best grade, while the student who knows the least gets the worst grade, the exam is valid. That's it. If an exam is not valid, nothing else—relevance, format, wit, charm, or DNA—makes the slightest difference. An invalid exam is a worthless waste of time.

A *valid* exam is not necessarily a *relevant* exam; in other words, an exam might be valid but not have any relationship to what has been taught. It is possible, easy, and pitifully common to design an exam that is simultaneously valid and hopelessly detached from what has gone on in the classroom. Happens all the time—most notably at the university level. An exam on shoelace tying, for example, is perfectly valid if the student who knows the most about shoelace tying gets the best grade. And if shoelace tying is what has actually been taught, the exam is valid and relevant, and bunnies dance in the meadow. Even if this test is given to a math class, it is valid as long as the student who knows the most about tying his shoes gets the best grade. The fact that it is so utterly detached from any known math program that it should be included only in standardized exams, where its foolishness will remain unobserved for generations, does not reduce its validity.

BAD QUESTIONS

Foul questions can damage a test's validity in a variety of ways. One way is by providing distractions and decisions unrelated to legitimate test-taking chores. When Student Smartz, for example, encounters a dumb question, she may be tempted to waste time wandering around in the intellectual weeds trying to make sense out of, and deciding what to do about, a fundamentally senseless question:

Question 19: Please explain why Beethoven's Third Symphony is bigger than his First and Second symphonies added together.

Student Smartz: This is a math test. How is question 19 related to math? I shall now waste several minutes trying to figure out what Ms. Hardscrabble has in her alleged mind.

Conversely, Student Dimbulb may not even see that there *is* a problem and simply plows ahead with legitimate, point-acquiring test-taking chores:

Dimbulb: What in the world is 19 all about? Who cares? Next!

Then to compound the problem, in a flash of compassion during the review process, Ms. Hardscrabble apologizes for question 19's lunacy and strikes it from the test—leaving Smartz doubly punished for wasting time messing around with what eventually becomes a nonquestion.

BAD FORCED-ANSWER ANSWERS

Not only can ill-conceived questions damage an exam's validity, but by diverting some students from productive test activities, improper *answers* on forced-answer questions can have the same effect. The problems can include

- Too few correct answers
- Too many correct answers
- Ambiguous answers

Improper answers often punish a student for knowing *too* much. Consider the following science true-false question:

True/False. Ignoring air resistance, a falling object will fall faster and faster.

The question is reasonable, but no unambiguous answer is provided. Some teachers, most students, and all administrators will agree that this statement is true enough for government work, but the student who has learned from unauthorized sources that the speed of light is a real-world limit is disadvantaged by seeing two right answers: the one she knows is right and the one she's pretty sure the teacher wants.

This changes the student's problem. Instead of selecting an answer based on her studiously acquired understanding of the subject matter, she now has to select an answer based on what she thinks the teacher has in mind. She can

- Waste time justifying to herself the need to choose the teacher's answer, or
- Mark the thing FALSE, thereby gaining a small personal victory while hoping for some justice and understanding during arbitration procedures—an iffy proposition.

Whatever choice she makes, by being diverted from legitimate test-taking chores, she is handicapped for knowing too much, and the exam's validity is damaged.

Similarly, how is a knowledgeable third grader supposed to cope with a science question that calls a daddy longlegs a "spider" or a scorpion a "bug"—when the kid knows better? As above, the student is punished for knowing too much.

(Actually, this is a bad example. In contrast to upper-grade students, third graders *know* what to do: start shouting. "Ms. Hardscrabble, question six stinks!" The college student thinks, "I can't make sense out of this question. Alas! There must be something wrong with me." School administrators think, "Let's set up a committee to explore alternatives to insects.")

Realistically, there is no way unfortunate questions and answers can be eliminated, but their numbers can be reduced by thoughtful consideration of each question and its attached answers at the time the exam is being written—a process that is most easily ignored in the design of essay exams.

BAD ESSAY EXAM "ANSWERS"

Essay exams and their marking are discussed at length elsewhere. Suffice it to note for present purposes that because these exams are inherently impossible to assess evenly, their validity is highly questionable. The problem is bad enough in K–12, and near fatal at the college level, with multiple readers and related pedagogical horrors.

WILINESS

Probably the most insidious, albeit entertaining, validity destroyer is wiliness. In a perfect classroom, two students with the same understanding of the subject would get identical scores. But things being as they are, some students unhampered by skill, understanding, or significant study too often get the better grades. These are the test-wily students who have learned how to get good test scores without going through the formality of learning very much. At the same time, their less wily colleagues, lacking the requisite flimflam skills, stagger along, always getting undeservedly lower scores, and always wondering why.

Test-wily students understand that two unrelated accomplishments are required to get good grades:

- An understanding of the course content
- An understanding of how to take tests, in other words—"test wiliness"

Prior to the exam, the student's prime objective is to learn as much of the course material as possible—to study. But once the exam is under way, the rules change and the primary effort should become using test-taking skills to best advantage. In a perfect world with its perfect exams, there would be no difference between these aims, but in the real world, miserable exams are scarcely rare and flimflam skills are always a consideration.

Consider: If the exam is bad enough, it will reveal nothing whatever of the students' mastery of subject matter. If, for exaggeration, the course is entitled *Post-Pluperfect Algae of the Sahara*, and the exam relates solely to *American Quilting Prior to World War II*, a sound understanding of course materials will have zero effect on the student's grade, and test-taking skills become the student's only recourse. The more perfectly an exam evaluates student understanding of what has been taught, the less important test-wiliness becomes.

So what's the teacher to do? Teach test-wiliness, of course. Without a doubt, the only way to ameliorate these effects is to teach test-taking skills right along with the other skills that are supposed to make the world a better place. As education is rumored to prepare students for life outside of academia's ivy-cluttered halls, and as testing is an increasingly common part of life outside those walls, an understanding of how the test-taking game is *really* played should be an important academic goal. Undoubtedly, a one-hour wiliness seminar (*How to Emerge Victorious without Actually Cheating*) can have a greater positive effect on student scores than ten hours of more traditional academic efforts—particularly in connection with standardized exams.

From an administrative viewpoint, increased student wiliness can have dramatic economic and career-enhancing consequences. It is obvious that a lot of money depends on how well the kids do on standardized exams. If school A, for example, teaches wiliness while school B does not, school A's kids will do better on standardized exams than school B's. Not only may this reduce financial concerns, but it also looks good to everybody concerned with appearances:

Board member: By golly, I thought my cousin would eventually become a good principal when we hired him thirty years ago. Now we finally have some proof.

The techniques of getting good grades without having learned very much are many, varied, and to a large extent beyond the scope of this book. Undoubtedly the best source of information on test-wiliness is the students themselves. Test-wily people generally have few reservations about sharing their particular collection of vile and effective test-taking gambits. The teacher who gets a classroom discussion started on the topic will be amazed, delighted, and possibly infuriated both by the suggestions that emerge, and for the obvious enthusiasm students usually have for a discussion of the topic.

Only a few possibilities are suggested here, but these illustrate the devious techniques some students use to triumph (partially and occasionally, anyhow) over the otherwise debilitating handicaps of not having bothered to study and/or poor tests.

- Try to determine the answer the teacher wants. Most of the time, the right answer and the answer the teacher wants are the same thing. But don't count on it.
- Never leave a question blank. Never. Forced-answer, essay, standardized, or anything else, a blank answer is always wrong.

- On all forced-answer exams, in the absence of any significant information regarding the *real* answer
  —First eliminate all obviously preposterous answers.
  —Then eliminate all the possibly preposterous answers.
  —If there are any answers remaining, employ "creative intuition"; that is, guess.
  —If this process of elimination eliminates all answers, start over and don't be so fussy.
- As discussed elsewhere, get the lowest grade possible on any pretest.
- Always read the questions and their answers with determination and skill. Then ignore one or both as appropriate. Instructions that prohibit guessing, for example, are to be enthusiastically ignored.
- On essay exams, if the correct answer is a mystery, "misunderstand" the question and provide a superb answer to the wrong question. What's to lose?

Question: When did Columbus sail the ocean blue?

Answer of Wily Student (who can't recall ever hearing of the date 1492): Columbus sailed the ocean blue during a period of fundamental change in Western thought. Added to technological advances in marine navigation . . .

Similarly

Question: Who is buried in Napoleon's tomb?

Answer of Wily Student (who is somewhat unsure what a Napoleon *is*): The French people are buried in Napoleon's tomb. Their hopes, their dreams, and their incarnadine passions are beneath the hallowed and verdured loam as surely as . . .

So okay. The kid didn't answer the question Ms. Hardscrabble thought she was asking, and as suspicious as Ms. H. is regarding hot-air artistry, the odds are that the kid will get more credit than none.

MINIMUM SCORES

There are occasions when wiliness backfires. Once upon a time, in the days of the military draft, a young man decided that his best chance of staying out of the army was to fail its true/false intelligence test—something not easily accomplished. By determined application of his ample intelligence, he managed to (a) get every answer wrong, and (b) find himself drafted within the week.

Why? A characteristic of forced-answer exams, unappreciated by all but the most test-wily student, is that the lowest possible score on any exam is not necessarily zero, but the score that one would expect to get without reading the questions. The lowest possible score on an essay exam is indeed zero, but the lowest possible score on a reasonably lengthy, reasonably well-written true-false exam is 50 percent. On a five-possible-answer multiple-choice exam, zero student comprehension is indicated by a grade of 20 percent. Any scores significantly below minimums should set off alarms like those caused by a sudden classroom silence. Better check it out. Something's awry.

What the draft board understood, and the sudden soldier didn't, is that it is exactly as easy (or as hard) to get 100 percent wrong on a true-false exam as it is to get 100 percent right. Either way, one must know all the right answers.

CHEATING

To the extent that it allows cheating, an exam is invalid. Cheating, in any of its vast multitude of forms, weakens an exam's validity as the student who is the more skilled and determined cheater has an advantage over the student who has directed his grade-enhancing efforts along more socially approved paths. Cheating tilts the playing field and muddies the teacher's perception of a student's understanding, which is, of course, precisely what the cheater has in mind. The last thing the cheater wants is a valid test. Further, the more expert the student cheating, the more difficult it is to detect. But all is not lost. There is a simple, well-proven method that will reduce the frequency and severity of cheating to near-nil: assure that it doesn't work.

What's the usual sort of cheating? Not peeking at another's paper. Peeking is obvious, uncomfortable, requires nearly superhuman eyesight, and assumes the peek*ee* knows more than the peek*er*. Peeking is out. Without a doubt, the most common, low-tech, cheap, and effective cheating method is the use of crib notes: those tiny little jottings in the palm of one's hand, semi-available on one's shoe instep, or hidden anyplace else that isn't hazardously conspicuous.

The form and location of "unauthorized reference materials" isn't so important to the present discussion as their content. Great dissertations on the "big ideas" test writers claim to test? Not a chance. Thinking back to your own crib-note-writing days, these testimonials to small handwriting almost never contain anything except trivia of the sort that, in real life, one looks up. Maybe a formula or two, perhaps a date, or maybe a handy mnemonic device. No grand ideas; after all, just how big is one's instep, how small is one's handwriting, how keen is one's eyesight? No crib note ever contained a "big idea."

Cheating most commonly occurs in closed-book, indirect exams. Cheating on open-book and direct exams is not much of a problem. Even the most creative and committed cheater realizes that there is little to be gained from the devious ploy. After all, how can you cheat on, for example, a tuba solo, with the whole world out there listening? This, of course, suggests the premier method of reducing cheating: make all exams open book. Encourage all students to thumb index their books, redo their notes, and create voluminous crib notes that address the grand ideas, the small ideas, and everything else the student thinks might be useful. As has been suggested, this sort of creative summation is often referred to as "studying," an activity often recommended by many educational authorities. Furthermore, it is an effective method of information management that will probably have ample rewards in the real world.

GUESSING

It can be argued that a good guess is a product of creativity, has many of the earmarks of inspiration, and is a short hop from genius. One of the characteristics that separate human thinking from machines'—at the moment, anyhow—is that we can make adequate decisions based on information that ranges from pitifully inadequate to essentially nonexistent. (Most politicians and many school administrators regularly base decisions on ephemera even when factual information is painfully obvious—but then, that is another matter.) In the absence of adequate information, life almost always rewards the astute guess, and the marvellous "leaps of logic" that humans can make should be encouraged at all times.

In spite of the fact that penalizing guessing always causes more problems than it solves, the EdBiz "literature" virtually oozes with clever methods of reducing, penalizing, or obviating guessing. The most probable reason for this foolishness is that guessing can mess up some of the statistical jiggery-piggery that those entrusted with analyzing standardized exams require to provide an appearance of social utility. But in contrast to many administrators' firm beliefs, the classroom teacher's primary testing concern is not increasing the statistical reliability of some externally imposed exam, but rather an attempt to evaluate her students fairly and efficiently.

Many classroom activities already encourage making decisions based on inadequate information—guessing. To a large extent, informed and experienced guessing is a fundamental requirement for all of the arts—musical, visual, verbal—whatever. Sports? Guessing what your tennis opponent or the opposing baseball pitcher has up her sleeve is part of the game, and he who guesses best may well beat the socks off an equally talented nonguesser. And relevant to current interests, guessing what particular items or concepts will be stressed on the next exam is a highly useful part of the test-wily student's toolbox.

Penalizing guessing always damages an exam's validity in that it penalizes and rewards students without regard to their understanding of what has been taught. Exactly as with cheating, and even with the most draconian off-with-their-heads threats in place, a good guess still provides as much benefit to the student as actually knowing the answer. Penalized or rewarded, some students are going to do it anyway, and the exam's validity is damaged. Furthermore, only bad guessing and inept cheating are punished. Do it right and you'll get away with it. And how's that for an upstanding life lesson?

Students who follow "no guessing" strictures get lower grades than students who don't. There are few teacher-generated noises more pleasing to the test-wily student than the announcement, "Now students, no guessing!" The savvy student, understanding full well that a no-guessing edict simply penalizes his classroom colleagues who are silly enough to follow foolish instructions, is going to guess big-time no matter what teacher says. The only realistic effect of "prohibiting" guessing is to punish the rare classroom inhabitant who actually follows instructions while rewarding the instruction nonfollower. This is not generally considered sound pedagogical methodology.

Mathematical penalties for guessing, such as one point for a right answer, zero points for a blank answer, and minus one point for a wrong answer, penalize the shy, hard-core direction follower, who, in contrast to the student who plows ahead with the "best guess" method, will only mark those questions that she feels have an unrealistically high probability of being right. Further, such penalizing schemes make exams slower to mark, increase turnaround time, and decrease teacher efficiency—all to punish those students who don't guess cleverly enough.

So what to do? Teach guessing, of course. If guessing is actively taught and encouraged as a part of the curriculum, rewarding the good guess increases both the relevance and the validity of the test. Decriminalizing guessing deprives the expert guessers of at least some the ill-gotten advantage provided by disapproved but highly effective guessing.

Heresy #1

Students should be encouraged to make the best guess possible—even when exam instructions claim a "penalty for guessing." The typical penalty is so slight that a student is likely to "break even" with totally random guesses and easily come out miles ahead with even moderately clever guessing. A blank answer is always wrong while a guess always has a better-than-zero chance of being right.

Heresy #2

Provide classroom exercises, specifically including exams, that require students to make decisions based on insufficient information—that is, to guess. Here are some examples:

Question: Three pets are asleep on a child's bedroom floor. One is a dog. Another is a cat. What is the third?

Question: The car won't start. Why?

As students generally have *some* information upon which to base an answer, totally blind guesses are rare. The student who has actually studied the material makes fewer guesses, and those guesses he does make are based on more information than the nonstudier—a double benefit. On a good exam, as in life, guessing will never beat studying. All else being equal, he who hits the books will always get a better grade than the guesser, but in school as in life, the student who studies *and* guesses will always beat the studier who declines to guess.

PRIOR INFORMATION

In connection with indirect exams, prior information can be a powerful lunch-hour study stimulant, at least for later-period classes. ("Gotta know this by sixth period or I'm morgue meat.") Consider the following common scenario:

- Suzy takes the exam first period.
- Suzy spills the beans to Mary.
- Mary finds time for serious study during the day.
- Mary takes the exam last period.

Cheating? Probably, in the sense that the students have been told not to do it, and if they do it well enough they won't be punished. The process certainly gives Mary an edge—exactly as Mary hopes. But a *validity* problem? No. Prior information may benefit later classes and skew somebody's bell-shaped curve, but the individual students are still evaluated on what they appear to know about the exam materials. Further, at the end of the day, Mary knows more about the subject than she would have—thanks largely to the fervent last-minute studying that prior information often inspires.

Prior information is seldom a problem with direct exams. The flute player, for example, knows perfectly well what's going to be on the exam—pucker and blow. And the question arises, isn't informing the students as to the contents of the next exam exactly what the teacher has been trying to do all along? Really snazzy teaching assures that all students are aware of what is going to be on the exam. What's the big secret?

SPOT-CHECKING

To reiterate ad nauseam, a *relevant* exam tests only that which has been taught. A seldom-considered additional requirement is that a *valid* exam must test *all* of what has been taught—not excerpts.

Time constraints often encourage teachers to resort to spot-checking. They attempt to evaluate student understanding by asking a few carefully selected questions and hoping that student response to these heavy hitters will reflect overall understanding so accurately that there is no need to address all of the important topics individually. Odd. This makes about as much sense as testing an arithmetic student only on subtraction, assuming that his addition skills are no better or worse, and entering an overall arithmetic grade in the gradebook based on this peculiar notion.

Exams that only sample parts of what has been taught have a large validity problem in that success on the exam depends too much on dumb luck. Students who study everything, as students are supposed to do, get the grades they deserve, while everybody else may get better or worse grades than deserved—all depending on luck. The student who is lucky enough to have studied the topics actually addressed will get a better grade than the student who, unluckily, studied other equally important but untested topics.

Two examples may illustrate the problem and emphasize the notion that teaching is best in the lower grades and degenerates thereafter. It is routine for a third-grade teacher to assign twenty spelling words, ask the kids to spell the words as she reads all twenty of them, and assign a grade based on the students' responses. No validity problem here; the student who knows the most gets the best grade, and Lady Luck takes a hike.

In contrast, the university History of Architecture professor assigns thirteen *Pre-Calderan Formation* churches, asks questions about three of them, and assigns grades based on this spot-checking. No good; too much dumb luck. The student who accidentally studied only the three asked-for churches will get the same grade as his more diligent colleague who studied all thirteen. Furthermore, the student who was unlucky enough to have studied only the ten unasked-for churches will get exactly the same grade as the student who studied none.

The problem seldom is that there is "too much to cover." The problem more often is that the questions are not carefully constructed. With the thirteen churches above, the question "What is the one significant structural feature shared by all of these churches?" might be relevant, useful, valid, and amenable to forced-answer formats. If the teacher wants to expand a bit, she might ask, "What is one significant structural feature shared by only three of the assigned churches?" Or a US history exam might ask, "What was the one significant domestic policy problem shared by the five assigned presidents?"

Of course, one may suggest that students can easily go around the problem of spot-checking and sampling by studying all important topics. True, and many outstanding students acquire outstanding grades by doing exactly that. But what outstanding students do doesn't change the fact that any exam that only *samples* student understanding leaves too much to luck and has a large validity problem.

NEW STUDENTS

Generally, the problem of new students is of no particular concern at the college level; colleges don't have new students. A student who shows up in the middle of the term will be told to take a hike. At the K–12 level, students show up early, late, or any other time, and the teacher is expected to be creative.

What to do? Considering the typical classroom constraints, probably the best the teacher can do is ask the new student to "take" the test. Doing so will give the new person something to do while teacher is highly involved with the other thirty-some students, provide him with a suggestion of what the subject matter is and how it will be evaluated, and give him a rich opportunity to explore the delights of the "'Aha!' phenomenon"—that is, how one can learn things from a test.

LANGUAGE-LIMITED STUDENTS

Students who have limited English skills pose a very similar problem. Various committees often enjoy calmly discussing the long-term problem—in the abstract and over coffee. In the classroom however, the kid stands there, waiting for some sort of instruction in some sort of language, and the teacher must cope, *now*—no abstractions and no coffee. With thirty or more other equally deserving kids in the class, and Open House tonight after this afternoon's faculty meeting, she copes. She probably asks this "pedagogical challenge" (possibly via crude pantomime) to "take" the exam. As long as everybody understands the problem and maintains near-zero expectations, the damage is minimal. Triage.

Note that his is not a trivial problem. Currently, Los Angeles, while probably being the second largest Spanish-speaking city in the world, is also host to a wide variety of students speaking over one hundred different languages in the home.

THE DISTRACTED STUDENT

Problems such as illness, hormone attacks, distracting personal problems—anticipation of feeding time, tight underpants, flatulent classmates, whatever—can easily prevent the occasional student from demonstrating his mastery of the materials on the test. Sad, but it happens to everybody at one time or another, and there isn't much the teacher can do about it. Subsequent to the exam, and at the risk of appearing to be a snoop, the teacher may want to investigate a little, with an eye toward understanding and possibly ameliorating the problem. But then, considering what the problem may be, she may not.

5

Design

Good design procedures are surprisingly universal. No matter the subject matter or grade level, somebody—the teacher, one hopes—decides it is time for a test, selects the exam format, decides on a bunch of questions, writes an even larger bunch of acceptable and otherwise answers, and eventually arrives at an exam that seems reasonable at the time. Just like that. Well—not quite. In the real world, there are many considerations that must be dealt with successfully if the resulting evaluations are going to have much value.

LOADING

One characteristic of every exam is its "loading"—a term that describes when the teacher puts in the greatest amount of time and effort. There are three kinds of loading: center, front, and rear. Most performance exams, including nearly all primary-grade evaluations, are "center loaded" in that they make their greatest demands on the teacher's time and expertise during the administration of the exam. The teacher observes a student's performance directly—perhaps watching little Alphonse attempt to resolve the BOYS ROOM/GIRLS ROOM dichotomy, or listening to a five-foot-nothing tuba player whack away at "The Stars and Stripes Forever"—and assigns a probably mental gradebook entry on the spot. Little teacher time is required to plan the exam, marking and ranking occur simultaneously, and posttest activities are minimal. Turnaround time—the time between the administration of the test and when the students get their results—is essentially zero.

Front-loaded exams make their major time-and-effort demand before the students see the test. Multiple choice and other forced-answer exams, with their up-front planning and design requirements, combined with speedy marking, are heavily front loaded. Front loading does not necessarily save time overall, but simply allows the teacher to invest time when time is rationally available. In addition to teacher convenience, front-loaded exams are generally preferred to rear-loaded exams for several other reasons. Front-loaded exams

- Encourage more thoughtful planning and preview
- Encourage evaluation consistency
- Provide very short turnaround times
- Provide more focused review

Rear-loaded exams make their major time-and-effort demands after the students are through with the things. Essay exams are almost always horribly rear loaded in that they can be quickly designed and assigned, but usually require long, late hours to mark—virtually guaranteeing geologic turnaround times. As they do not *require* adequate planning or preview, the teacher often remains unaware of exam glitches until after the exam has been administered. Then it is too late. The review of rear-loaded exams too often consists of little more than the teacher defending poor questions and answers that proper planning would have prevented. About the only nice thing that can be said about rear-loaded exams is that they make front- and center-loaded exams look good.

STATUS/PROGRESS

One of the eternally attractive Teachers' Room discussion topics is whether students should be graded on

- Progress—how much information the student has derived from the course—where sweet Alphonse is now compared to an earlier time, or
- Status—the student's total understanding of the subject matter up to the time the test is given—where Alphonse is now.

PROGRESS

As the alleged goal of education is to prepare the student for life, and as life is seldom interested in where or how one has learned anything, classroom time spent assessing progress is largely wasted. One may be hired on the basis of a resume filled with references to where and when all manner of wonderful learning supposedly took place, but the real world's approval, on-the-job success, bulging bank accounts, and personal satisfaction generally stem from what one knows at the moment. Nobody much cares where or how Einstein learned what he learned or how much he improved between the ages of five and seven. Being told that the brain surgeon was the most improved student in her class is unlikely to spread cheer among her patients:

> I'm sure her mother is proud, but what does Dr. Triplethumbs know *now*?

To evaluate student progress, two exams are required: a pretest given before instruction, and a posttest given after instruction. The theory is that if the pretest score is subtracted from the posttest score, one arrives at a number that is supposed to have some relation to the student's progress. While this procedure has provided a shaky basis for generations of EdD theses, it has one benefit and several wishfully fatal flaws. First the bad news:

Beyond the obvious drawback that two exams use up twice the classroom resources as one exam, if students are going to be graded on the difference between their pre- and posttest scores, the exams must be identical. Any variation between the exams will destroy whatever value the clumsy procedure is intended to provide. This in turn mandates a level of planning and curricular rigidity that doesn't often, and probably should never, exist in a real classroom.

Sorry, kids. I'm sure you find this morning's capture of our understandably hysterical principal by bug-eyed aliens mildly interesting, but as little green men weren't on the pretest, they won't be on the posttest. So let's just return to the fascinating subtleties of the post-participular orthogenic elliptical gerund.

Then there is the entertaining certainty that once the test-wily students understand how the pretest/posttest game is to be played, they can be counted on to employ massive, creative, justifiable, and highly effective fakery.

Okay, kids. I'm going to ask you to do all the push-ups you can now, and again at the end of the semester. Then I'll grade you on how much you have improved.

Sure thing, Coach. The test-naive kids will give it their all—sweating, groaning, whimpering—while the test-wily students, making the same pitiful noises, will get the tummy off the tarmac exactly once. And who, if graded on progress, will get the best grade? Not the dimwit that did 100 push-ups in September and 120 in June for a 20 percent improvement, but the smarty-pants who did 1 at the start and 20 at the end—neatly netting a grade-enhancing 2000 percent improvement while doing 119 fewer pushups than his sweatier, less test-wily colleague.

The process of pre- and posttesting presents an additional problem of the sort that can drive teachers into rational employment. If the same exam is given to the same students only a day apart, with no intervening instruction, most posttest scores will be higher than their pretest counterparts simply because the students are familiar with the questions. All students' scores? Not a chance. As surely as coaches shout, there will students whose posttest scores will be lower than their pretest scores. Go figure.

So what's the good news? A pretest can serve as an elegant introduction to forthcoming studies:

Okay, kids. Here is the sort of exam, and the kinds of questions, you can count on when we finish this unit. This exam won't count on your grade, but it will help make the new material more understandable.

So if attempting to assess progress is wasteful, counterproductive, or impossible, what's left? Status: how much does the student know about what has been taught.

STATUS

At first glance, efforts to evaluate status appear to run head-on into the eternally vexing educational problem of gigantic, untidy, and inconvenient student differences. All working teachers routinely expect new students to pour through the classroom door with vastly different talents, training, and DNA helices. Unless carefully structured, status-only evaluation procedures can produce some peculiar results. If the puny, immature little PE student is evaluated solely on number of push-ups or baskets scored per game, he is unlikely to get any grade higher than F+. Conversely, the preadolescent Superkid will get all As, without lifting one genetically programmed, muscle-bound finger.

The obvious way to avoid this pedantically counterproductive situation is to keep firmly in mind that a relevant exam measures what one wants to know. Chances are that what the curriculum dictates, hence what the teacher generally wants to know, is not the status of the student's muscle mass or her ability to actually see over, and make pleasant noises on, a snare drum. Chances are the student should be evaluated on her status regarding musicianship, sportsmanship, teamwork, and other fuzzily defined and hard to quantify attributes, the evaluation of which has inspired many teachers to seek career reassessment counseling.

EXAM PREVIEW

Exam preview is the attempt to find and fix as many of the exam's problems as possible before the exam is administered. Regardless of format, adequate preview can improve the exam's relevance and validity, reduce its rear loading, expedite its marking process, and greatly enhance the teacher's overall effectiveness and emotional well-being.

Inadequate preview too often results in off-the-cuff exam assignments for which the teacher has no firm idea of what student responses to expect, and even less notion of what responses she will accept. Run a topic up the flagpole, observe what sorts of salutes appear, and only then decide which salutes are acceptable. While the surprises inherent in this approach may provide a welcome diversion during late-hour marking sessions, the approach hardly assures that students focus on big ideas or that anybody gets his depths of understanding probed.

The preview process is not difficult, probably taking less time to do than to read about. One thinks up a hopefully serviceable question and previews it with regard to several criteria:

- Format. Is this really the most appropriate format? Indirect? Performance?
- Utility. What is the true function of this question? Is it a straight shot at determining who knows the most and who knows the least? Maybe it is a quite legitimate teaching tool, passing along some information—curricular or otherwise. Perhaps it is simply a means of acquiring defensive gradebook numbers, or as is most likely, some combination of these functions.
- Clarity. Will the students understand what the teacher thinks the question asks—no tricks, ambiguity, or inappropriate language?
- Relevance. Does the question address what really has been taught?
- Validity. Is the student who knows the most likely to get the best score? It may be useful to use a couple of well-known students as bellwethers. "If there is any chance," mutters the test-writing teacher, "that Alphonse gets this right while Suzy gets it wrong, the question and/or its answers have big validity problems."
- Difficulty. Is it likely that everybody or nobody will miss this question? Will there be adequate time for a thoughtful response?

An interesting extension of exam preview is to try out questions and possible answers on the entire class before the exam is administered. "Here are the questions I may ask you next Thursday. What can you find wrong with them?" Or perhaps, "I'm open to suggestions. What might be a dandy distractor for the first question?" This pretest effort can be a fantastic teaching opportunity, and a marvelous opportunity to help students focus their studying.

WEIGHTING

The simpler-the-better bookkeeping that most teachers strive for might seem to be an unlikely spot for subjectivity to enter the testing process. Well . . .

All bookkeeping systems add more than a little subjectivity through the process of weighting—deliberate or otherwise. Deliberate weighting is the process of adjusting gradebook entries to better reflect whatever the teacher has in mind:

> Lessee. If I ask more or less the same question five or six times, it just might soak into a few student heads that either I think this represents an important point—or that I've finally lost all my marbles.

The other kind, accidental weighting—is the process of doing nothing and letting nature take its course. Accidental weighting can lead to some peculiar results. For example, the English composition teacher who records student essay letter grades "as is," implies that all essays are equally important: that a dinky one-paragraph assignment should have as much effect on the semester grade as a ten-page term paper. The teacher who counts and records the number of correct answers on forced-answer tests inadvertently weights each exam according to the number of questions on each test. By doing nothing, Ms. Hardscrabble allows a forty-question exam on addition, for example, to have twice the semester grade impact as a twenty-question exam on subtraction. A hundred-question history exam on the evolution of the flea collar industry will have ten times the semester grade impact as a ten-question exam on the Civil War—as well as make it clear that Ms. H. suffers from some badly skewed priorities.

In spite of the fact that it can complicate and slow the test-writing procedure, deliberate weighting may be called for. One easy way to weight is to enter an important exam's grades into the gradebook more than once. If the teacher decides that the term paper is three times as important as a paragraph, she simply enters the paragraph's grade into the gradebook once and the term paper's grade three times. Or with point scores, the teacher may choose to multiply some scores by a convenient—and completely subjective—correction factor:

> Aha! If I double everybody's subtraction score, lambs will cavort in the meadow and all will be well.

Or, as with letter-grade scores above, she can simply enter the numerical grades into the gradebook twice. Awkward, but in the absence of better up-front design, this weighting will assure that subtraction and addition skills, for example, affect the semester grade equally.

POP QUIZZES

> Experience may be the best teacher, but her pop quizzes can be killers.
> —Anonymous

Pop quizzes are far more common than generally realized. They are the lifeblood of directly evaluated classes:

> Johnny, please draw me a horse.
> Suzy, please demonstrate a *glissando poco triblastissimo* on your trombone—gently if possible.
> Alphonse, please . . . (significant pause) . . . Oh, forget it.

One common justification for pop quizzes is that they encourage the students to "keep up" with their studies. But one wonders how important—

outside of a study habits class—this "keeping up" is. While it is probable that such exams tend to punish the students who study at the last minute while rewarding the students who keep up, so what? Does it really matter when a student studies? As "keeping up" is unlikely to be part of anybody's curriculum and has not been taught, it is ultimately irrelevant. So why reward it?

Pop quizzes' quick and easy design too often encourages their completely unacceptable use as an emergency classroom control technique. Many teachers, perhaps goaded into folly by a particularly vexing class, have been known to use an off-the-cuff essay assignment as a classroom tranquillizer. ("There's nothing like a good 500-worder to calm the cretins.") While such professional foolishness may be briefly effective, after the triggering crisis has passed, the teacher must decide what to do with the resulting pile of essentially pointless, unmarkable manuscripts. As actually reading the stuff is obviously out of the question, an alternative must be found. A morally reprehensible and effective solution is to dump the entire mess into a wastebasket, vow to never become similarly entrapped, and get on with education.

REUSED EXAMS

Yessir, our teachers are so good they only need to write one or two tests throughout their entire careers. Ms. Hardscrabble's exams, for example, still prohibit the use of slide rules—whatever *they* might be.

Consider the probably untrue story of the college freshman who, finding a severe need for a dynamite, scholarship-retaining essay, digs into his fraternity's file of oldies but goodies, jobs off a reasonably good copy, and hands it in—uncharacteristically on time. When the essay is eventually returned, our hero is stunned to see his effort inscribed with a large letter F and the comment, "I thought this was a lousy paper when I wrote it in 1872, and I still think it stinks."

The most obvious benefit of reusing exams is to reduce teacher workload—not necessarily a bad idea in itself. Testing is only one of her numerous classroom activities, and time spent on any one activity is time unavailable for others. If teacher time spent creating tests can be reduced without harm, reduce it.

By using the same exam more than once, the teacher can more easily note long-term trends in teaching effectiveness. Invalid, irrelevant, or otherwise misbegotten questions probably have been eliminated in the first eight or ten years, the marking procedures have been refined and streamlined, and subsequent ranking may (but probably won't) benefit by comparing the current class's performance with that of a larger group.

Old exams are a fine source of both kinds of questions: good and bad. A seldom exploited use for old exams is to hand them out to the entire class as study guides—even if open-book exams are anticipated. This serves the same function as the frat's essay file, except the whole class benefits, not just the hard-core test-wily student who accidentally has a colleague who took the course earlier and saved the exams. But on the whole, reusing entire forced-answer exams, word for word, creates more problems than it solves. Simply reprinting exams eliminates any possibility of forced-answer open-book exams. Reused exams encourage cheating on closed-book exams as surely as many faculty meetings cure insomnia.

If exams are to be reused, the teacher is obligated to collect exams after review which, of course, precludes the students having access to their own exams for study or review. Silly and counterproductive. Furthermore, reused exams imply a rigid curriculum structure, with all the inherent problems that assure, and virtually require "teaching to the test." After all, if the exam is already written, it is only fair to the students that the instruction and class materials prepare them properly.

One may note that the State of California recently used the same standardized exam two years in a row and is pleasantly surprised to see how much the students' scores have improved. Of course, nobody would sink so low as to "teach to the exam." Of course not. Surely no. That would be illegal, immoral, unethical—and very effective.

Perhaps the most significant objection to reused tests is "How good is the thing anyway?" Is it so perfect, so marvelously relevant and valid, so accurate a reflection of this semester's classroom activities, so exquisitely discerning that it simply cannot be improved? Not likely.

6
Open-Book Exams

Okay, here we go: a little pedagogical heresy. As schools are supposed to prepare students for life, and as life's evaluations are almost always open book, all school exams should be open book—all levels and all subject areas. All.

CURRENT USAGE

In the real, nonschool world, there is little distinction between open- and closed-book evaluation procedures. When the Man with a Badge pulls one over and suggests one's speed was perhaps a bit excessive, he does not much care whether one looks up one's answer in a book or not. When the boss serenely asks, "What the hell did you do *that* for?" it is generally understood that an impromptu oral presentation is expected—*a cappella* and *con brio*—and if the forthcoming reply is improved by reference to a book, so be it. Having a rule book in his pocket is unlikely to be of much utility to a third baseman when he discovers that both the pitcher *and* the second baseman are simultaneously throwing a ball at him.

A few professions—law, real estate, education, and so on—require passing a closed-book exam before one is allowed to work. But once the bar exam, for example, is passed, that's *that*; the professional is unlikely to face a closed-book exam again. Closed-book driver's license exams are an attempt to assure the state that the applicant understands selected parts of the vehicle code. But even after demonstrating adequate performance on the exam, the driver's day-by-day activities are still controlled by such subtle open-book instructions as "STOP," "DETOUR," and the always catchy "WRONG WAY."

Many time-dependent "exams" such as emergency procedures might be considered closed book, but while prior-to-need awareness and hands-on practice are certainly preferred, one is *allowed* to research the operation of a fire alarm during a raging building fire. Big red letters: "PULL HERE, DUMMY."

Suggesting that all classroom evaluations should be open book really isn't calling for much change. Our earliest learning efforts—potty training comes to mind—are relentlessly and gratefully open book. In the early grades, evaluation efforts in all subject areas generally remain open book, not because little kids are illiterate (which they are) or because nobody has taught them the delights of cheat sheets (which nobody has), but because "looking things up" is a skill that deserves being taught in the early grades.

But as one moves along, evaluation in many subject areas becomes increasingly impersonal, and evaluation methods become increasingly closed book. The teacher starts covering up the map in the front of the room during a geography test, taking down the periodic table during a chemistry test, and locking up the dictionary. And, of course, any student caught using open-book reference materials during a closed-book exam will be severely shot. Sad and educationally counterproductive.

OPEN-BOOK EXAM CONSTRUCTION

Open-book tests may require more up-front time and thought on the writer's part, but the format does indeed encourage teachers to write questions aimed at assessing the student's grasp of basics and fundamental big ideas rather than easily researched trivia.

Often the only difference between open-book and closed-book exams is that open-book exams start with the word "why" rather that "what." Most students quickly appreciate that no self-respecting open-book exam is likely to contain the question, "What is the capital of California?" Too simple, too memory driven, too easily looked up, and too unrelated to any known big idea. Far more useful might be the concept-dependent question, "Why is Sacramento the capital of California?" Similarly, the closed-book chemistry question, "What is the atomic number of delirium?" is a waste of everybody's time. Whether or not a student happens to remember delirium's whatzit won't shed much light on her understanding of any chem course's big ideas. A far better question might be, "Why does delirium have the atomic number it has?"

As an additional plus, a trivial question accidentally included in an open-book exam is of little consequence. The student simply looks up the trivial answer to the trivial question and moves on. No great loss. In contrast, and as will be discussed later, a dumb question on a closed-book exam can cause real problems.

OPEN-BOOK EXAM VALIDITY

Keeping in mind that a valid exam gives the best grade to the student who knows the most about the materials on the test, open-book exams tend to be more valid than closed-book exams. How? By making easily researched trivia equally available to all students, open-book exams reduce the advantage memory experts have over their less memory-blessed colleagues. Further, open-book exams eliminate the problem of a missing, easily referenced bit of information interfering with a student's effort to make clear her understanding of larger issues. Much of what one hopes students have learned about chemistry, for example, cannot be rationally evaluated unless the students have test-time access to a variety of tables. To exaggerate considerably, note the trig student's plight:

> Student: Rats! If I had but memorized the entire trig table out to a few dozen decimal places, I would know the inverse haversine of

thirty-seven degrees and would be able to display my exemplary understanding of the right triangle. However, denied this essential bit of trivia, I am, trigonometrically speaking, dead.

Or consider the architectural history student's trial:

Question: Please explain the religious influences apparent in the design of Santa Maria della Lasagna.

If the function of the question is to explore the student's mastery of painfully memorized and easily forgotten trivia, the question—closed-book—couldn't be better.

Student: Rats! Never heard of the place. Next question!

But if the question really is an attempt to assess the student's understanding of religious influences on church architecture, certainly a "big idea" by anybody's architectural standards, the same question, open book, will encourage the following scenario:

Student: Rats! Never heard of the place. Gotta look it up.

Student dips into her carefully organized reference materials, notes that SMdL is a member of a group of churches that she *has* studied, and responds:

SMdL is a justifiably obscure example of pre-Carboniferous, post-Nasal Renaissance structures whose major design features include excruciating pew design, abysmal acoustics, and mushroom-encouraging ventilation. Furthermore . . .

STUDY HABITS

It will come as no surprise to note that research skills are increasingly vital to success in many real-life fields. Reference materials are there to be used, and the students should have access to all appropriate reference materials at all times—exactly as in the real world. The easy availability of computerized reference minutiae makes their acquisition so easy that their pretest acquisition becomes less and less of an end in itself. Freed from this chore, students have been known to devote more study time to a course's larger concepts. Heresy.

Students will study for the sort of exam anticipated, and if an upcoming exam is advertised as being open book, it is difficult to *force* students to study trivia. The dimmest bulb in the class is unlikely to waste much time memorizing the periodic table, the dimensions of twenty-three Santa Maria della Pasta Linguini churches, or anything else instantly available at the touch of an ENTER key.

One highly effective studying technique that open-book exams make possible is to ask the students to make up miniscule cheat sheets—of the sort generally considered cheating and consequently punished, if discovered. If these crib notes are required to fit on a three-by-five-inch card, for example, the students will be strongly encouraged to condense and summarize their information:

> Mercy. There is no way I can cram everything I don't know onto one crummy little three by five. Lessee. If I know formulas A and B, I can generate formula C and don't need to write it down. But then if I know A and C, I can generate D, and ... Actually, when I think about it, if I know A, I can generate all the needed formulae—and I already know formula A. A miracle! No more crib notes! Wow! Have I ever outsmarted Ms. Hardscrabble this time!

The process of reducing course material to its essence is often called "studying"—an activity widely approved of in many academic circles.

Similarly, open-book exams can prod the student, in the process of deciding what reference materials might be useful, to review what has been taught:

> Lessee:
> Periodic table? For a history exam?

Textbook? Don't think I ever got one.
Notes? Dog ate them—both pages.
Laptop? Nope. Batteries died last month.
Lady Chatterley's Lover? Unlikely utility.

One of the entertaining features of open-book exams, at least to the proctoring teacher, is how they inspire different student test-taking behavior. A student who has studied generally keeps her nose in the exam papers and only occasionally consults her carefully organized reference materials—with, as Mark Twain has said, "the serene confidence of a Christian holding four aces." The other student who, knowing the upcoming exam would "only" be an open-book exam, didn't bother to organize her reference materials, can be seen frantically pawing through great masses of illegible notes and other stuff—all panic, sweat, and futility.

"'AHA!' PHENOMENON"

Most students are sincerely motivated while searching reference materials during an open-book exam and generally learn more than anticipated. Even the most diligent and hard-studying student is quite likely to discover new information during open-book exams—an opportunity typically denied him by closed-book exams.

Interestingly, the student who has failed to study often benefits more from the "'Aha!' phenomenon" than does his more studious colleagues. During a closed-book exam, there he tranquilly sits staring at the questions as if they were written in Medieval Erse—accomplishing nothing. During an open-book exam, however, in a frantic effort to avoid academic Armageddon, he may actually learn something while thrashing through the available reference materials. He may still flunk, but even if he knew nothing of the material going into an open-book exam, he is sure to know something coming out.

CHEATING

Cheating is most effective, easily accomplished, and commonly encountered in connection with closed-book exams, notably those exams that emphasize memorized trivia. This is neither unexpected nor particularly reprehensible. If schools urge students to focus their study on the big ideas and then test on minutiae, schools get what they deserve. Happily, most students tend to realize quickly that cheating on an open-book exam is largely a waste of test time.

It should be noted that not all memorization is a complete waste of school time. Such things as definitions, the alphabet, the necessity of reading from left to right and top down, and a multitude of other arbitrary, agreed-upon "facts" must be memorized. In the mid-acne years, it is important to remember one's own telephone number, and in later years, remembering where one put one's car keys can be a challenge for some superintendents. But while many things indeed need to be memorized, most are effortlessly memorized by repeated use.

It may be useful to add a small caution regarding any sudden classroom switch from closed- to open-book exams. The first few open-book exams in a class that has little experience with this format may not be as valid as one might like. For example, the student who has acquired a fine grade point average by memorizing vast amounts of little things may need to experience a few open-book exams before he changes his study habits to take full advantage of the new situation.

7

Performance Exams

Basically, there are two kinds of exams: performance and indirect. Performance exams should be the testing weapons of choice whenever possible—all classes, all levels.

In contrast to indirect evaluation methods in which the student is asked to respond to questions *about* a subject, performance exams ask the student to *do* whatever it is he is supposed to have learned—exactly, one notes, as does life. The ceramics student throws a pot, the math student illustrates her mastery of square roots by manipulating square roots, the public speaking student speaks publicly, and the German student confronts the umlaut *mano a mano*. Even those paragons of indirect evaluation, multiple-choice driver's license exams, are usually combined with some sort of once-around-the-block performance test:

> Just show me that you can park it a short walk from the curb, off the sidewalk, while making as few loud noises as possible.

It is interesting to note that the techniques used to teach a kindergartener how to write an upper case letter A and those used to teach a naval carrier pilot how to land on a moving runway are essentially the same: one on one and performance oriented. The sophistication, penalty for failure, and cost to the taxpayer are vastly different, but the teaching method is the same.

RELEVANCE

As with most classroom concerns, the design and administration of appropriate performance exams is not always simple. In many subject areas, the teacher's primary task is to teach attitudes, understanding, and appreciation of a subject area. For example, in most districts the PE teacher's primary job is to teach and evaluate such life-enhancing and sweat-free attitudes as sportsmanship, fair play, teamwork, and an appreciation of others' excellence. As a consequence, Coach Jacques can not rationally assign grades on the basis of push-up–doing, hurdle-jumping, or even pitiful groaning. Counting sweat drops might be simple and satisfying, but by ignoring what supposedly has been taught, the resulting evaluation would be hopelessly irrelevant.

Similarly, the most relevant test of a clarinet student's understanding might seem to be to ask the student to whack away at Mozart—right in front of the grade-assigning teacher and a gaggle of giggle-repressing peers. And if the teacher's primary task were to help the clarinetist to blow the reed well, such testing methods would be deliciously appropriate. But in an attempt to avoid the problem of students entering a class with vastly different backgrounds and native talents, common sense and most curricula require the students to be evaluated on less obvious criteria—perhaps musicianship, teamwork, and an appreciation of peer performance. While actual performance on the instrument is commendable, it probably should be a small part of the grading scheme. "Virtuosity is its own reward," or something like that.

VALIDITY

Performance exams are almost always wonderfully valid. By allowing the teacher to observe and evaluate student mastery firsthand—with nothing intervening between student understanding and the teacher's perception of that understanding—the student who knows the most usually gets the best grade. Furthermore, even world-class test-wily students often find that their lovingly nurtured hot-air skills are largely useless in performance exams, and they are forced to demonstrate what, if anything, they have actually learned of the course materials. Sometimes it can be fun to watch the baloney artist sweat and squirm.

EFFICIENCY

With almost no effort other than to avoid making obviously idiotic assignments—asking the flute player to do push-ups, for example—performance exams virtually design themselves.

As observing and ranking are usually accomplished simultaneously, these exams enjoy the delights of center loading. The teacher observes the student do whatever she is supposed to have learned, and makes a gradebook entry of her completely subjective evaluation of how well the student measured up:

> By golly, that was the niftiest *Ode on a Grecian Grapefruit* I've heard a first grader recite all week. Grade of A for sure, for sure.

Direct testing can be surprisingly efficient even with some large-group classes. The choral music teacher, for example, doesn't spend much time planning, administering, or marking exams, but rather, she performs the remarkably classy feat of identifying, listening to, and evaluating an individual singer's performance, attitude, and understanding while simultaneously directing and listening to a large group of singers. Similarly, many band instructors routinely pick an individual instrumentalist out of the classroom's sonic chaos, listen to, and evaluate the student's response to instruction as if it were a one-on-one exam.

Interestingly, the same question can be either performance or indirect depending on the intent of the course. When a history student is asked to write a paragraph about King Olav the Obtuse, the resulting paragraph is an indirect method of assessing how much the student has learned about justifiably obscure royalty. One hopes that "history-irrelevant" considerations—handwriting, syntax, grammar, spelling, and so on—will not affect the student's history grade. But when the identical assignment is given to an English composition student, the resulting paragraph is a performance of what it is he was supposed to have learned about English composition, and his grasp of historical niceties should be irrelevant. The history teacher hopes to evaluate the student's understanding of history by means of an indirect written assignment, while the composition teacher asks the student to perform: to *do* what the teacher hopes his student has learned. Same assignment, different course intent, hence a different test type.

DEFENSE

Unlike most indirect evaluation methods, performance exams seldom provide a tidy paper trail of gradebook numbers that can be used to justify letter grades. As a consequence, and as discussed elsewhere, many teachers resort to devious, irrelevant, and highly effective stratagems which do nothing except provide columns and rows of solely defensive gradebook numbers. Points may be awarded for such ephemera as "classroom involvement" or "classroom contribution." Art students may get points for cleaning up the mess with some regularity. PE students are rewarded points for not wearing stridently aromatic sweat socks, and chemistry students may win numerical praise for leaving the building standing. While these efforts certainly are commendable, they are scarcely related to curricular "big ideas," nor have they been taught with any significant enthusiasm. Their ultimate utility of their official-looking numbers is to lend an aura of mathematical precision to an inherently imprecise process. Good enough.

OKAY, SO NOTHING'S PERFECT

While it has been suggested that performance exams should always be the format of choice, it is obvious that some subjects simply are not amenable to this format. History, for example. As a complete reconstruction of World War II is most certainly beyond the resources of the most exalted university history classroom, the student is unlikely to be asked to "do" World War II in the sense that a welding student is asked to weld. For all the entertainment value inherent in such an approach, the teacher will probably have to give up on full-scale reenactments as being far too expensive and noisy, and settle for indirect, paper-and-pencil evaluation that he *hopes* will provide adequate insight into student mastery.

8

Forced-Answer Exams

There can be little argument that at all levels and in all subjects, performance exams are the academic weapons of choice—when possible. Simply ask the student to demonstrate how much he knows about what has been taught. Sadly, such exams are not always possible, and the teacher is forced to choose between two format possibilities: forced-answer and essay. Many teachers resist using forced-answer exams because, to the extent they prohibit variable student response, they allegedly fail to explore adequately the student's understanding of what has been taught. Slander. The inference that essay exams actually do explore the depths of student understanding is, of course, nonsense.

It probably is worth noting up front that all forced-answer tests are actually true-false tests. All forced-answer exams provide the student with one or several possible answers that the student must rate as acceptable or otherwise. Each provided answer must be judged on its own merits, one at a time, as true or false.

It also may be worthwhile to note that all forced-answer exams have one more option than is usually granted them: the blank answer. In fact, a true-false exam might more properly be known as a "True-False-Huh?" exam. Blank answers have some significant implications to the grading process and are discussed elsewhere.

UNIFORMITY

In contrast to essay exams, all students take the same forced-answer exam—more or less, anyhow. With essay exams, the student who accidentally (or otherwise) misunderstands the question is free to wander off into the weeds attempting to answer an unasked question. And then, of course, the marking teacher has the jolly tasks of puzzling out what the question *is* that the student thought he was answering and evaluating the student's response to that question. Too much for the midnight hour. Conversely, in a forced-answer exam, the student who misunderstands the question is unlikely to find an appropriate answer and is forced—like it or lump it—to go back, reread, and reevaluate the question's meaning.

SUBJECTIVITY

One quality of forced-answer exams that virtually all EdBiz literature finds good and virtuous is their "objectivity." As usual, the EdBiz literature is wandering around in its limited-reality world. As discussed at length elsewhere, forced-answer exams are exactly as subjective as all other exams: completely. Exactly as with all other formats, all forced-answer questions and answers are decided upon by an actual, highly subjective person. Live with it.

"'AHA!' PHENOMENON"

With essay exams, the information is almost exclusively *from* the student *to* the exam paper. The student is asked a question, and he responds with all the information he has available, almost never learning anything from the exam.

With the acceptable answers printed right there on the paper, forced-answer exams can be delicious teaching tools—at least with students who are test-wily enough to take advantage of this characteristic. The student reads the question; even if she doesn't know the answer offhand, she can gently tease out the question's real meaning by reference to the provided answers:

Student (to herself): This question doesn't make sense. Let's take a look at the answers. Okay. If question eighty-seven means blah blah blah, then—aha!—answer D is correct. I didn't know that, and now I do. How marvellously educational. Next!

Chances are that in the process of reading the possible answers closely and deciding which one the teacher is most likely to prefer, the student will learn something. It will never beat studying, but every little bit helps with some students. And perversely, the less a student knows about the subject coming into the exam, the more he will benefit from the "'Aha!' phenomenon."

The "Aha!" benefit is not reserved for students. In the process of bouncing back and forth between questions and answers, the test-writing teacher is forced to review the questions and their potential answers with a level of sincerity rare in other exam formats.

VALIDITY

Some EdBiz literature suggests that because the students can respond to more forced-answer questions than essay questions in the same length of time, forced-answer exams can explore a far greater *range* of student understanding. Again, pooh. The range and depth of student understanding is assessed not by the number of questions, but rather by the quality of the questions. Several dozen trivial questions will only result in several dozen trivial answers.

As with all other formats, forced-answer exams are exactly as valid as their questions and subsequent marking allow, but by reducing the test-wily, hot-air artists' irrelevant strengths, forced-answer exams can do much to assure that the student who knows the most about what has been taught gets the best grade.

In the effort to reduce the effect of blind guessing and to assure that students who know the answer to an important question get ample credit, well-planned forced-answer exams often ask the same (rephrased, perhaps) question more than once. The chances of correctly guessing the answer to a true-false question, for example, is one out of two. The "same" question asked three times has one chance in eight of being guessed correctly. All of which, to the test-wily student's disgust, increases validity; it puts a large premium on actually knowing some right answers.

Forced-answer exams are much fairer than essay exams to students with language problems. The student only needs to comprehend the question, and while that may be a daunting task in itself, the student isn't further handicapped by the need to make his understanding clear in some "foreign" language.

(It probably is worthwhile to reiterate yet once again, one more time, the notion that the number one, primary, and most important skill American education can engender is a mastery of English. With it, all else is attainable; without it, the student is in trouble deep. As important as other subjects may be, they should never take priority over English.)

DESIGN

The benefits of forced-answer exams don't come for free. Forced-answer exams are the most difficult and time-consuming of all exams to write. Not only does the teacher have to think up clear and discriminating questions, but she must also devise clever and unambiguous, possible-but-wrong "distractors"—a task that takes time and patience to do well. The right answers must be right at all times and under all circumstances, and the distractors must be wrong at all times and under all circumstances. Neither right nor wrong answers should include giveaway clues, such as the words "always," "never," or "all," nor should there be any correct-by-default answers such as occur when all other answers are transparently goofy.

Total teacher time required to write *and mark* forced-answer exams is far less than with essay exams. Furthermore, as their time-eating planning and construction efforts are accomplished before the tests are administered, forced-answer exams benefit from the delights of front loading, and their turnaround times can be marvellously short—

perhaps measured in seconds. Good. Got other things to do. Teaching, for one thing.

Bad forced-answer exams are almost as easy to write as bad essay exams and generally deserve the reputation of being a lazy teacher's friend. One simply selects a series of true statements regarding the subject at hand, and then messes up about half of them. Here is an example of such inexcusably easy, dumb, and essentially useless true-false questions:

CALIFORNIA HISTORY CLASS EXAM
Example 1
True/False. Sacramento is the capital of California.

Note that with this type of question, the student who knows absolutely nothing about the topic can expect to get full credit half of the time, while his colleague who has studied can hope to get one point on every question—*if* he makes no mistakes. Little validity.

Additionally, this sort of question has zero "Aha!" content—the student learns as much from it as from an essay exam—essentially nothing. If the teacher really wants to test the student's understanding of whatever it is they have been studying, she's going to have to work a little harder on the questions and answers. She probably should avoid easily researched "what/where" questions and go more for "why" questions, such as "Why is the capital of California, Sacramento, located where it is?" rather than "Where is the capital of California?"

Example 2
The capital of California is located in Sacramento because

A. It has an excellent seaport.

B. The people in charge hoped to isolate the new capital from anticipated population centers.

C. It is at the intersection of two major rivers.

D. Located high in the mountains, the site assures nifty TV reception.

E. The people in charge wanted to locate the capital as far away from San Francisco as possible.

F. The people in charge wanted to locate the capital in a beautiful redwood forest.

Notice that the best an absolutely clueless guessing student can hope for on this type of format is one correct answer for every six questions—far greater validity than Example 1 above. Although there may be a small amount of "Aha!" content, the typical student procedure on questions of this sort is to read down the list of available answers until the "right" one appears, mark that answer, and go on to the next question—neglecting to read, or benefit from, the remaining possibilities.

A far better format might be as follows.

Example 3

The capital of California is located in Sacramento because

1. *True/False. It has an excellent seaport.*

2. *True/False. The people in charge hoped to isolate the new capital from anticipated population centers.*

3. *True/False. It is located at the intersection of two major rivers.*

4. *True/False. Located high in the mountains, the site assures nifty TV reception.*

5. *True/False. The people in charge wanted the capital to be as far away from San Francisco as possible.*

6. *True/False. The people in charge wanted the capital to be in a beautiful redwood forest.*

Here the committed guesser can expect to get three correct answers no matter how he marks them, while the maximum a studying student can acquire is six. Obviously, this format does not have the hard-nosed validity of Example 2, but it provides enough other benefits to compensate for the lack.

Unlike the previous examples, this format strongly encourages the student to read *all* of the available answers, and to benefit thereby from whatever "Aha!" content there may be. It allows the teacher to "weight" questions to reflect her (subjective) idea of their importance. If the teacher doesn't think the question has a six-point value, for example, she can provide more or fewer possible answers.

GRADING

The typical multiple-choice grading procedure is to run off a copy of the exam on stiff colored paper, cut holes on the right answers, and lop off the corner where the kid is asked to write his name. When grading time arrives, the teacher scans each paper for multiple answers, slaps the template on the individual student's paper, counts and marks the right answers, writes the grade on the student's paper, and enters the grade in the gradebook.

This process is fast, easy, only mildly boring, and even allows a little student/teacher interaction even if the kids don't know about it:

Let's see. Next paper. Hmmm. Suzy's. Wonder how she did?

For the really stout of heart, one may refrain from marking the wrong answers, leaving that information for the review process.

Review Period Scenario 1

Alphonse gets his paper handed back with wrong answers and final score plainly marked. Sweet Al quickly checks the teacher's arithmetic (as well as he is able), mutters to himself that he may be in big trouble at home, and goes to sleep. No review for Al. Why bother?

Review Period Scenario 2

Alphonse gets his paper handed back with only the raw score noted. "I was robbed! I can't possibly have missed that many—no how! Just wait! I'll show Ms. Hardscrabble what's what!" And then Sweet Al pays uncharacteristically close attention to the complete review session— perhaps actually learning something in the process. "Hmmm. I think I see why I missed that one. Hmmmmmm." Fantastic learning experience. And isn't that what school is all about?

What to do when a student changes an answer or two and sweetly asks the teacher to change the grade? In reality, this is not much of a problem, but for the benefit of hard-case students, Ms. Hardscrabble may elect to photocopy selected students' test pages before they are returned to the students.

An accusation regularly leveled at forced-answer questions is that they too often are graded by machines. Transparent slander. No machine has ever graded an exam—forced answer, essay, performance, standardized, or personal hygiene. The probable reason for this peculiar objection to forced-answer tests may be confusion between grading and box counting. With delightful precision, objectivity, and speed, grading machines simply do as they are told; they count the number of properly filled-in boxes. Deciding which little box is the proper one remains the teacher's job. Grading requires human input, which in the case of forced-answer exams, occurs up front, during the exam's design and preview.

Grading machines generally require answers to be marked on a piece of paper separate from the test sheet. This requires the student to split her attention between pages—an unappreciated distraction that makes it easy for a student to accidentally "skip" an answer. The result is that all following answers do not respond to the questions the student has in mind. In addition, the answer sheets are not exactly cheap. A thirty-student class can go through $10 of grading machine answer sheets in a remarkably short time.

REVIEW

Review of forced-answer exams can be a relatively straightforward, no–lesson-plan class period. As each question has a strictly limited number of possible answers, the entire class's efforts can often be reviewed in a reasonable length of time. The teacher makes clear what she intended each question to ask, what sorts of answers she anticipated, and stands back to let the discussion roll. With any luck, the teacher quickly becomes an underpaid moderator:

I hear your point, Suzy. What do you think about it, Alphonse? Alphonse? Yoo-hoo, Alphonse?

DEFENSE

One of the distinct advantages of forced-answer exams is they can generate a large number of semi-fraudulent gradebook numbers that can be used to justify almost any grading process—even including completely subjective assignment of letter grades. While these numbers are exactly as subjective as those in all other formats, they look like they represent something substantial and "objective."

9
Essay Exams

Everybody knows what "essay exams" are. They are those long-winded, ambiguous-response, language-dependent exams that require complete sentences—platoons of properly arranged nouns, adverbial clauses, and other linguistic mysteries. They are those exams with geological turn-around times—and yes, neatness counts.

Some of the original enthusiasm for the format may fade in the first few years of teaching, particularly among teachers who develop a low pain threshold for late-hour paper-marking sessions, and those whose assigned subject matter stubbornly resists evaluation via essay exams. But many teachers are content to go along with the familiar process, teaching as they were taught: think up a few probably ambiguous questions, administer the exam, somehow evaluate student essay responses in one or several late-night efforts, and agonize over resulting grades.

And these teachers have allies in high places. Much of the EdBiz literature makes impressive claims regarding essay tests' efficiency, efficacy, desirability, and moral superiority—somewhat akin to TV late-night snake-oil infomercials but without the laughs. As is often the case, the literature is all wet. Typical essay exams are the most overrated and inefficient evaluation instruments ever invented. They are infested with so many inherent flaws that their use should be banished to some obscure academic island where they won't attract attention or frighten small children. Unfortunately, we're often stuck with them.

RELEVANCE

The most important advantage claimed for essay exams is that they allow examination of student understanding in great detail—really dig in and plumb the old depths—to allow the teacher to assess student comprehension of fundamental principles with objectivity, lucidity, and compassion. Nonsense, of course. One wonders what subjects essay boosters have in mind—math, PE, art, physics, literature? Essay exams are appropriate only to a narrow range of subjects. Very narrow. One: English composition.

Lest anybody go into professional shock regarding the above, it is vitally important to note that language skills are the most important and pivotal of all school subjects at all levels. With adequate ability to read and write, all other areas of learning are accessible, and if a student lacks these skills, all the time and effort necessary should be devoted to their acquisition, even at the expense of all other subjects. But this does not suggest that the needed instruction should be sneaked into nonlanguage classes. To the extent that language skills have not been taught, they are irrelevant. To the extent that they fail to differentiate the students who know the most of *what has been taught* from those that know the least, they are invalid.

Downgrading an art student, for example, because of nonart literary inadequacies—creative spelling, pathetic grammar, Sanskrit-like handwriting, or nonexistent keyboarding skills—makes no more sense than punishing her for lack of athletic ability or dental hygiene. A sensitive awareness to the semicolon may be rewarded in heaven or in Ms. Hardscrabble's English composition class, but it should remain irrelevant to the student's grades elsewhere. As sensitivity to English syntactical nuances and elegant handwriting are neither required to understand history nor have they been taught in the history classroom, they should not be allowed to affect the evaluation of a student's history expertise.

"Yes but," one hears from the back row, "what about physics? Physics requires some level of mathematical skill. How is that different from requiring some level of language skill for success in history?"

Easy. Mathematics is *the* language of physics; without adequate math skills, the student is not only unable to show what he knows on an exam, but he is also unable to comprehend the subject matter. Just as one can have a world-class understanding of history, physiology, architecture, elementary trombone, or almost any other subject without understanding a word of English, an understanding of physics requires an appropriate level of math sophistication.

There's a time and place for most things. The teacher who fiddles around playing volunteer English comp teacher, hoping to enhance the English comp skills of non–English comp students, does so at the expense of what she is being paid to do. One wonders whether the most effective venue for teaching language skills is, for example, an anatomy exam. The time a political science professor spends redlining a student's poisonous spelling is time unavailable for legitimate, assigned subject matter. No matter how virtuous the intent, she has less time to plan, teach, and evaluate what she is supposed to plan, teach, and evaluate. As difficult as it may be for many teachers ("Just *look* at all those filthy, dangling, postprandial participular phrases! Where's my red pencil?"), the effort must be made to evaluate student performance only on truly course-relevant accomplishments.

In all fairness, such clear-headed discipline is not easy, and at the very least, inadequate language skills can easily color the teacher's perception of student understanding. To herself: "Anybody so stupid as to regularly split infinitives, as this student tends to so often do, can't expect to really get good grades." In the extreme, if the student's English language skills are so dismal that Ms. Hardscrabble can't understand what the student is trying to say, she can scarcely be blamed for thinking "To hell with it," and taking off on an extended bicycle tour of the Lesser Antilles. Nor is she to be chastised for reluctance to assign grades to things she can't read:

> Look, kids. In marking this exam I'll try to ignore disgusting language skills, but don't expect much credit for anything I can't read—and yes, neatness counts.

The literature often suggests that essay exams encourage students to study the larger relationships. More nonsense. In an understandable effort to avoid academic disaster, students will indeed study for the sorts of exams anticipated—open book, direct, multiple choice, driver's license. It is not the exam's format that encourages the study of big ideas, but rather the student's conviction that as surely as coaches shout, big ideas are going to be on the next exam.

Conversely, if a teacher's exams are noted for their shallow and trivial questions, that is precisely what will be studied. All that can be claimed with any certainty is that the prospect of an essay exam will encourage students to study for an essay exam—perhaps to the extent of brushing up on one's high-speed handwriting.

Essay exam boosters occasionally suggest that essay exams can be useful in identifying students with language problems. Here they may have a trivial point. However, this identification function generally is a solution in search of a problem. Identification only has to happen once, and most students with language difficulties and a little bit of luck are well identified early into their academic career—perhaps three minutes into an astute teacher's classroom. Language difficulties, while certainly demanding prompt and comprehensive attention, are seldom considered late-breaking news to subsequent teachers.

If essay tests are so misbegotten, why are they so common? Perhaps the biggest reason for their use is because so many teachers are at ease with them, finding them familiar, comfortable, and traditional. This is not surprising, as essay exams have been good to most teachers. A major requirement for becoming a teacher is to demonstrate above-average success on essay tests over many school years, and many teachers have fond memories of those classes in which essay exams played a major role:

> Essay exams allowed me to demonstrate how clever I am, and I'd like my students to have the same opportunity. After all, what was good enough for me sure as hell is good enough for the collection of nitwits I face every day. And anyhow, that's what teachers *do*.

In addition to tradition, familiarity, and inertia, a common reason for using essay exams is their ease of design. They are *so* easy to think up. Nothing to it. Juicy topics virtually leap to mind:

> *Please describe World War II in precise detail. In order to keep your response focused on essentials, please ignore Germany and Japan. Yes, neatness counts.*

But ease of design may cause more problems than it solves. Importantly, essay exam designers often find it easy to shortchange effective preview options. Feeling a need for, and/or having threatened the students with, an exam tomorrow, the teacher writes a few questions that seem reasonable at the time and goes back to red-inking the pile of essay exams that has grown like three-hole fungi since the third day of the semester. Sadly, she only becomes aware of the rotten apples in this latest exam during some dismal late-night marking effort—when it is too late to make repairs, corrections, or amends:

> Thank goodness essay exams are so easy to create. I'm so busy marking essay papers into the wee hours of the morning that I just don't have time to design exams that obviate marking essay exams into the wee hours of the morning.

BAD QUESTIONS

While bad questions are inevitable in all formats, they do more damage in connection with essay exams that with other formats. It's simply a matter of percentages. As forced-answer exams usually have more questions than essay exams, one or two bad questions on a true-false test will be less damaging than the same number of stinkers on an essay exam. To exaggerate, if an essay exam has three questions and three of them are bad, that's 100 percent, and the exam should be discarded as unfit even for student consumption. However, if a forty-five question forced-answer exam has the same number of clinkers, that's only 7 percent, and while nobody is particularly happy about the situation, the flawed forced-answer test certainly is more useful than its flawed essay colleague.

AMBIGUOUS QUESTIONS

Ambiguous essay tests can raise silliness to new heights. Ms. Hardscrabble means one thing when she writes the question, but Suzy, perhaps in all sincerity, understands the question to mean something altogether different. Come marking time, Ms. H. not only has to evaluate how well Suzy answered the question, but she also has to puzzle out what the question *is* that Suzy answered. This is not necessarily an impossible task, but with several such answers on an exam and the classroom-typical number of exam papers, the process does take time. Much time. Which is one large reason why Ms. Hardscrabble seldom returns essay exams quickly enough for them to have much currency or utility.

Ambiguous questions place an emphasis on wiliness. Some students are rendered mute, helpless, and nonproductive by unclear questions:

> Oh dear me. I don't really understand what Ms. H. has in mind. It must be my fault. I guess I'll just sit here and feel guilty.

Others, the test-wily students, view vague questions as a challenge. As high adventure. As daddy's credit card.

> Oh man! Lookee at all that indecisive ambiguity! I trust my hot-air skills remain unblunted by any foolish and obviously inappropriate study efforts.

The student who legitimately misunderstands an essay question won't know he even had a problem until so informed by colleagues at lunchtime, and then it is too late.

Please explain the causes and effects of the Battle of Bull Run.

Student Jose, not having read the assigned chapter and only fleetingly perplexed about why Ms. Hardscrabble included such an odd question in an American history exam, prattles on at lucid length about the annual Running of the Bulls in Pamplona, Spain.

When Ms. H. finally gets around to marking the paper, she is forced to spend too much time trying to fathom what the student thought the question was asking. Eventually she

- Puzzles out what the question apparently meant to the student,
- Notices that his understanding of certain cultural customs is outstanding and that the unasked question is superbly answered,
- Says "to hell with it" and books a six-week winter skateboard tour of Tierra del Fuego.

OVERLY BROAD QUESTIONS

In an attempt to "cover" a significant part of what has supposedly been taught, and in the absence of adequate preview, the questions may become self-defeatingly broad, unfocused, and essentially unanswerable:

Please describe the worldwide acquisition, manipulation, delivery, utility, and historical relevance of food. Feel free to use the margins of this paper if you need more room. Neatness counts.

Poorly defined questions allow too much room for students to (legitimately or otherwise) answer different questions. This in turn makes uniform and focused review very difficult, slows the marking process to a crawl, and plays into the hands of the test-wily.

TOO MANY QUESTIONS

Too many essay questions in any exam put a completely irrelevant and invalid emphasis on speed. Considering the fact that an unanswered question is always wrong, while a poorly answered question is generally worth more than zero, the faster student gets more answers on his paper and has a better chance of a better grade than does his slower colleague. And since when is handwriting speed relevant to anything?

"'Aha!' Phenomenon."

Except when they are open book, essay exams provide essentially zero "'Aha!' phenomenon"; students rarely learn anything in the process of taking the test. In contrast to forced-answer exams in which several possible answers generally assure that students will learn *something* from the test, the flow of information on an essay exam is almost completely *from* the student *to* the paper. Whatever the student knows about the subject going into the exam is very close to what she'll know coming out.

MARKING

Teachers who choose, or are stuck with, essay exams probably go through the least entertaining marking process in all of education, and some level of masochism is both useful and customary. Red pencil at the ready, late hour, depressed by the entire concept, the teacher plows through a vast pile of semilegible, quasi-literate papers, struggling to evaluate student understanding in a reasonable, consistent, and useful manner.

Not only does the appalling process of marking a few dozen papers on the same topic have a profoundly warping effect on the human brain, but every paper is evaluated by a slightly "different" teacher. Suzy's exam is marked in the middle of the afternoon by a teacher in one state of mind/exhaustion. Johnny's effort is marked at midnight by an entirely different teacher. Martha's effort gets a fast shuffle ten minutes before class on the day the papers are to be returned, and because her teacher always arranges the papers in tidy, gradebook-accessible alphabetical order, Cindy Zzych is in real trouble.

As students present creative or unanticipated answers, the marking person's notion of acceptably correct answers often changes during the marking period. Consider the following scenario. In the middle of an all-night marking session, Ms. Hardscrabble notes that Alphonse has, contrary to all expectations, brought up an excellent point unaddressed by the preceding essayists. Alphonse's point is so well made and germane that Ms. H. should properly go back and reassess all of the previously marked papers. Is she likely to do so at 2 A.M.? Of course. Surely. You bet. All papers marked after Alphonse's utterly atypical flash of insight will be marked with his offering in mind. Those marked prior to that remarkable event are most *un*likely to be reviewed and remarked.

Student brilliance is not the only cause of this sort of problem; teacher misjudgment can suffice. Consider the teacher's dilemma when, as the papers crawl past, she realizes that almost none of the students has understood a point that she thinks important, well taught, generally understood, and for the lack of which all prior papers have been downgraded. Obviously something's fishy with the question, but go back and reassess all of the papers? Of course. Certainly. When pigs fly.

No doubt the worst essay exams occur in connection with large college classes where class size itself can make essay exams unacceptable and inappropriate in all subject areas. As it is absurd to expect one person to read and evaluate several hundred essay exams in any Earth-planet timeframe, "readers" are hired to do the job. As it is equally absurd to expect the readers to evaluate the exams in any uniform way, many professors resort to having the readers look for and count the "key words." This simply changes the exam from an unmarkable essay exam into an unplanned, awkward fill-in exam.

It has been suggested that computers will have come of age when they can recognize your mother with a new hairdo. Close, but no cookie. Microchippery will have truly arrived when computers can properly evaluate an essay. Computerized essay exam marking would certainly solve a lot of problems—uniformity, short turnaround, speed, ease, fraudulent aura of objectivity—all those nifty things. But computers being such as they are now and likely to remain, and even if they were able to fathom handwriting, or if all essay exams were entered via keyboard or voice, it is hard to imagine essay exams ever being machine graded this side of the Pearly Gates. Essay exams must be graded by hand now, and probably always will be graded by hand—slowly, painfully, subjectively, arbitrarily, and nonuniformly.

REVIEW

Essay exam review is a slow, usually boring process that often leaves many students unclear of where they went wrong—or right, for that matter. As most questions can be interpreted in a few dozen ways, and every student provides a unique set of answers (or had better!), the time required for effective review is not generally available. Consider the numbers. Fifty-minute class period, thirty-five students answering a half-dozen questions, some time out for teacher to explain his view of the questions, some time for debate, and probably some additional time lost while the administration spends a few minutes on the PA system extolling the cafeteria's lunchtime delights . . . Not much time. About the best Ms. Hardscrabble can do in the time available is to address the most-missed questions in the broadest of generalities. No wonder students go out the door still unsure of why they got the grades they did.

DEFENSE

All teachers' grading systems are subject to attack, and teachers who rely on essay exams to provide a major part of their evaluation schemes are particularly vulnerable. No matter how fraudulently acquired, numbers have an aura of respectability, authority, and objectivity, and Ms. Hardscrabble may want to convert letter grades to number grades as early in the process as possible. An effective method of accomplishing this change is the infamous "Backwards System" in which the teacher, after informing the students of the upcoming deception ("Okay, kids. I consider a grade of 90+ to be some sort of A."), assigns a numerical grade even if a letter grade is what she really has in mind.

And lest we forget, lots of red marks also can help confuse the issue. A student whose paper is covered with juicy red marks and assigned a C grade is far less likely to complain than the student whose paper has no marks on it and is assigned a C. You can fool some of the people some of the time—and that's usually good enough.

FILL-INS

Fill-in exams are those short-winded ambiguous-response exams in which complete sentences are neither expected nor appreciated. The student just puts down a word or two in the typically inadequate space provided and hopes that they are the same word or two the teacher wants. Fill-ins don't offer any of the benefits essay exams allegedly provide nor do they offer any of the efficiencies inherent in other indirect exams.

As student answers almost never match teacher anticipations, the problem of ambiguous student responses is particularly acute with fill-ins. Whenever the marking teacher confidently awaits the appearance of the word "run," for example, as surely as tacos leak, she's going to have to take the time to decide whether "trot," "campaign," "encompass," "operate," "manage," "flow," or any other student-provided synonym will suffice. It is one thing to "suspend" misbehaving students, but "hanging" them probably isn't what is intended—no matter the provocation.

To fill-ins' credit, rotten language skills are unlikely to have as much impact on the teacher's perception of student understanding as with essay exams. Further, these exams are less tolerant of the hot-air artist than full-blooded, verbs-required essay exams. After all, how much puffery can even an expert cram into a single word? Puffery requires the sort of literary elbow room provided in abundance by essay exams. Fill-ins are much easier to mark and as a consequence have shorter turnaround times than their long-winded relatives. They are the only acceptable format for spelling tests and might provide useful format variety—but then so might a short musical interlude or a summer vacation.

10
Grading

Once the exam has been designed and administered, and individual student performances have been noted, three additional steps are required for an effective grading program: ranking, reporting, and reviewing. Ranking is the process of comparing a student's performance to some standard. Reporting is the process of providing the People Who Count (PWC) with some sort of meaningful indication—a grade—of the student's performance. Taken together, Ranking and Reporting add up to Grading.

As is often the case in educational activities, the process of grading is best accomplished in the primary grades. At this level, most grading is one-on-one, nose-to-nose, hands-on, and letter-grade free. No true-false exams, no essays comparing and contrasting Nietzschean ethnological differences between, for example, LEFT and RIGHT. The teacher simply teaches the functionally illiterate little kid what she is supposed to learn, observes how well she has learned whatever she is supposed to have learned, discusses her status with her—and keeps moving.

While this probably is the ideal method of evaluation and grading, it only works with little kids who haven't encountered the depressing fact that life and school generally reward and punish on the basis of relative performance. Sooner or later, Alphonse and his parents are likely to become dissatisfied with the vague evaluation that Alphonse "is making fine progress" toward understanding and acting on the difference between the GIRLS room and the other one. Eventually comparisons need to be made: Ranking is required. As Alphonse's mother might ask,

> Tell us, Ms. Hardscrabble, is it customary for a kid of Alphonse's age to get it right all the time, most of the time, or only as rarely as our son accomplishes this socially significant task?

RANKING

Effective grading requires that student performances be ranked: individual performances must be compared with some group. With the sorts of exams that result in a large collection of numbers—multiple choice comes to mind—this is reasonably simple. The group to which the individual student's score is compared is simply everybody who took the test.

The process is less clear with exams that do not result in a pile of what one hopes are significant numbers. Essay exams come to mind. Imagine *identical* paragraphs submitted by three students. How good is the paragraph? Depends. If one writer is a first-grade student, the teacher may decide that the effort is superb. If the second student is a sixth-grader, the paragraph might be judged as being about average. The same paragraph written by a college senior would probably merit a decidedly dismal grade. In all events, student efforts are assessed in the context of some defined group.

REPORTING

Once ranked, the results need to be reported. A useful reporting system has two basic requirements. First, it must reflect the fundamental accuracy of the teacher's testing methods. A pass-fail system suggests that the teacher's evaluation methods are accurate enough to support this reasonably crude, two-rank system—a fairly safe assumption. As grad school applicants often must have a "B or better" to be accepted, and as only undergraduate As and Bs add up to "pass," the system obviously is a two-pigeonhole, pass-fail system.

Returning to Alphonse and his struggles, whether his parents are aware of it or not, they are quite clearly asking Ms. Hardscrabble to report Sweet Al's ranking in an understandable, three-pigeonhole format: "all the time, most of the time, or rarely." A "straight percentage" system is a 100-pigeonhole system that claims to be so marvellously precise that student performance can be divided into 100 discrete pigeonholes—that a grade of 75 is significantly different from a grade of 74 or 76. Some standardized exams claim to accurately place the students into 1600 discrete and meaningful pigeonholes. Not likely.

CLARITY

In addition to reflecting the fundamental accuracy of the teacher's testing and evaluation methods, a useful reporting system must make the teacher's evaluations clear to the PWC. As long as their meanings are clear to the PWC, what the pigeonholes are called is not important. A system that divided student performances into groups called Rats, Snails, and Puppy Dog Tails would be a perfectly satisfactory three-pigeonhole system if the grade of Puppy Dog Tails meant anything whatever to the PWC. Again, unlikely. (It has been reported that the next to worst grade a naval carrier pilot can acquire upon landing is called "Dinky"—DNKY—"Damn Near Killed Yourself." The worst grade is usually accompanied by organ music, tears, and lamentations. One notes that these grades are very well understood by the PWC.)

As an entertaining example of how things can go wrong, the State of California recently urged,

> In place of grades, teachers should monitor student growth in terms of a child's placement on a performance curve rather than on a sterile grade."

They further encouraged teachers to

> Consult a five-point scale of descriptors from beginner to fluent reader.

In an attempt to go along with whatever it thought the state was trying to say, one school district instituted a system that ranked student performances as Independent, Confident, Capable, Developing, Limited, and Emerging. Eventually it occurred to somebody that these "descriptors" just might not be universally self-evident, so the district created an official "Handy Reference Guide" to accompany each report card. This guide explains, for example, that an "Emergent" reader is one "who does not have the ability to read print independently." Indeed.

Other than the always appreciated light humor they provide, such state-sanctioned urgings are worse than useless. Not only do they invite endless semantic warfare over the differences between "Confident" and "Capable," but by violating the requirement that all grading systems must be understood by the PWC, they make exposition of student performance more difficult than it already is. The chances of a grade of "capable" meaning the same thing to the teacher, student, parents, and everybody else are nil—with or without a Handy Reference Guide.

WARM FUZZY REPORTING METHODS
There are several basic reporting systems in common classroom use today. Perhaps the silliest scheme attempts to measure student performance against some sort of fuzzily defined personal standards—not even the teacher's fuzzily defined standards, but the student's fuzzily defined standards:

How do you *feel* about the book you claim to have just read?

While sweet Suzy may be proud as a clam for actually having read an entire book without help or cheating, whether she is forty-two years old and the book is *House on Pooh Corner* or three years old and the book is *War and Peace*, her personal evaluation is unlikely to impress anybody except her parents. While a clear appreciation of one's strengths and weaknesses certainly is useful in life, as with many other aspects of formal education, it will net one a cup of coffee only when accompanied by cash. Self-satisfaction—or self-criticism, for that matter—had best be its own reward, because external rewards are rare.

BELL-SHAPED REPORTING METHODS

Other common losers are those grading systems that attempt to rank a student's performance in relation to some "absolute" standard. One such, the Good Old Bell-Shaped Curve, requires that the students' performances fit into some preconceived pattern. ("By all that's standardized, there *will* be 10 percent As—or else!") While this statistical curve may be useful in other contexts or in any group that indeed has exactly 10 percent outstanding students—neither 9.9 percent nor 10.1 percent—it is inapplicable to any Planet Earth classroom.

One of the several unexpected consequences of this sort of "kids fit the curve" program occurs in connection with advanced-placement courses. For example, the decision is made to offer an advanced physics class for those students who might benefit from it. Who are these students? Typically they are those who have been getting As in science all along and would almost certainly get an A in the existing class. The advanced class is offered, the students benefit from it, and when report card time rolls around, the official grading policy dictates that only 10 percent of these otherwise straight-A students can be given an A. Then as surely as all computers hate all humans, the following semester's advanced class will contain exactly zero (voluntary) students.

FANTASY REPORTING METHODS

Similarly, many districts encumber themselves with district-wide absolute grading standards that make it convenient for the teacher to make foolish decisions. These standards often are the result of long-forgotten faculty meetings and have never been employed or reconsidered. One such is the "90–100 percent=A, 80–90 percent=B" fantasy. This charming pedagogical artifact assumes exam questions can be so elegantly crafted, so exquisitely relevant and valid, that a grade of 90 percent is a perfect A-, while 89 percent is a perfect B+. Additionally, this scheme suggests that every teacher in the entire district can provide dozens of such evaluative jewels each semester. How amusingly smug.

To the extent that any reporting method fails to consider the classroom variables that effective evaluation must take into account—teaching and exam quality, attendance, student tracking and preselection, phase of the moon, hormonal imbalances, and so on, it is unlikely to accomplish anything useful. But all is not lost. It must be noted that inappropriate systems can be, and generally are, discarded without the least twinge of regret when they produce a grade spread that some highly subjective person doesn't like. For example . . .

FUDGE FACTOR REPORTING METHOD

Early in their teaching careers, many classroom teachers encounter and overcome the problems inherent in absolute grading systems by employing a variety of creative ploys. One such device, the widely used but seldom discussed "Fudge-Factor" system works like this. The teacher writes his first exam, administers it, marks it, and is suicidally depressed to note that the *highest* score is 37 percent:

Oh, what a dreadful teacher I am! Oh, what a sorry collection of witless cretins that class is. Woe!

Then reality sets in:

There is simply no way that any (much less all) of those brilliant, hard-working, potential Nobel Laureates could fail any exam. Nor am I *that* rotten a teacher. There is something fishy here.

Right. Something is. After significant soul-searching, angst, and mathematical trial and error, the teacher stumbles onto the officially nonexistent "Fudge Factor" grading method. In a flash of insight, he discovers that by adding a carefully calculated fudge factor to everybody's score ("61 points should do the job"), he will get a grade distribution more to his liking ("Not too many As, not too few Cs, juuuuust right"). While this approach is crude, slow, and may cause the teacher to suffer a few pangs of guilt ("If I were a real teacher, this subterfuge wouldn't be necessary"), it maintains a smoke-and-mirrors connection with official policy—and it works.

BACKWARDS REPORTING METHOD

The related, disapproved, reprehensible, and highly useful "Backwards System" is often used to circumvent the silly. The teacher evaluates a student's effort and decides on a letter grade—D+ for example. Referring to the official "90–100=A" rule book, she notes that "67=D+", and she enters the *numerical* value into the gradebook. Totally subjective, philosophically questionable, quick, and simple, this system has only the vaguest connection with any board-approved absolute system. But what the hell: without wasting too much time and effort, it allows the teacher to remain in control of the evaluation process, makes clear her perception of student performance, emits an aroma of objectivity, and provides defensive gradebook numbers.

> Parent: How come my precious daughter got a D+?
> Teacher: Because her paper got 67 points.
> Parent: Oh. I see. Thank you for making that clear. Please accept these two tickets for an expense-paid week in Paris as a small token of my appreciation and esteem.

In all fairness, absolute standards, bell-shaped or otherwise, can provide a few noneducational benefits. They are simple enough for many administrators to understand, they look nice on EdD theses, they spice up administrative reports to the board, and they are easily defended. ("Gee, I don't make the rules. I just follow them.")

A GRADING METHOD THAT GENERALLY WORKS

So, having explored what doesn't work, what does work? What's a hardworking teacher to do? Considering the estimates, approximations, and subjective decisions present in all evaluation processes, the system that probably makes the most sense to most people is the familiar ABC system. If pluses and minuses are not allowed, this is a five-pigeonhole system. If such are allowed, it becomes a twelve- to fifteen-rank system—depending on whether such intellectual arabesques as "F+" are acceptable in polite society.

SCATTER MAKING

Ranking is most easily accomplished with tests that provide the teacher with tidy rows of numerical gradebook scores—forced answer, mostly. If the gradebook contains letter grades instead of numerical grades, she might be well-advised to convert them by assigning four points, for example, to all A grades, three to the Bs, and so forth. Then all that she needs to do is to arrange the scores in some sort of vertical scatter.

The highest number of student-acquired points goes at the top, along with a tally mark for each student getting that score. The smallest number of student-acquired points goes at the bottom along with a tally mark for each student acquiring that miserable score. Any well-trained computer can do this in a couple of jelli-seconds, and even doing it by hand is not a major project.

With sixty-five students taking the exam, one might get something that looks like this:

37 ll

36 lll

35 ll

34

33 lllll

32 lllll ll

31 lllll l

30 IIIII III

29 I

28 IIII

27 IIIII I

26 I

25

23 III

22 IIII

21 II

20 II

19

18

17

16

15 III

14

Then one simply grits one's teeth, grasps one's pencil firmly, and (while ignoring the screams of outrage from non–classroom types who aren't faced with the problem, aren't required to solve it, and have no better suggestions anyhow) draws lines between the As, Bs, Cs, Ds, and that other grade. That's almost all there is to it. Decide and draw the lines.

"Almost?" Indeed. The resulting grades still need to be reviewed—subjectively, of course. Who got the top grades? Who got the lowest? How about the kid with language problems? The new kid? How come the usually top kids did not generally get the top grades? How in the world did Alphonse actually get a B while Suzy got a D? Where are the lines drawn if the grades are part of an advanced-placement class? Where are the lines if the class is a remedial class? If it has been decided to use a two-pigeonhole, pass-fail system, where do the lines go?

This method works as well with report card grades as with individual exams. With the numerical grades tidily scattered and the lines drawn, the teacher notes the semester grade the system suggests assigning to each student, and then, with supreme subjectivity, decides if the suggested grade is the best grade for each individual student. What about the kid with the lowest grade? Who is he? Maybe checked into class only yesterday, or perhaps has been absent for some time, or is afflicted with other unique problems. Is it fair or simply stupid to give him the F he apparently deserves? With a smile on her face and warm feelings in her heart for all humankind, the teacher raises, lowers, or leaves grades as is according to her experienced judgment. Actually, rather fun.

11
Posttest Activities

Note that many states have laws prohibiting anybody, in the absence of fraud or error, from requiring a teacher to change a grade.

As has been discussed in relation to specific exam formats, and while review efforts vary among exam types, several review functions apply to all formats. Perhaps the most important use is to make clear to the students what (in the teacher's subjective opinion, of course) each question was intended to ask, and why one answer is more acceptable than others.

"BUT YOU TOLD US . . ."
Another benefit of effective review is to encourage feedback from the students to the teacher. For example, what to do when a student has found a legitimately improper question—too few or too many answers perhaps? One approach which, if nothing else, will keep many students focused on the review process, is to give credit to the *first* student to point out the problem:

> Right! Good answer. I didn't think of that when I wrote the question. You get full credit. When we finish, remind me and I'll change the gradebook.

Of course, at this point fully half the class will leap into the air:

Me too! Me too!

To which the teacher will reply:

Sorry, people. The rules have been explained. The *first* person to note a bad question gets the credit.

For a really foul question, one that is so far off the mark that the teacher wonders how it sneaked in, the only solution is to discard the question for the whole class. But of course this approach creates the problems of punishing the students who wasted exam time trying to understand the question only to have it become a nonquestion, and the need for additional teacher time spent fooling around with the gradebook.

Whatever the exam format, the teacher can maximize the review process's time effectiveness by making a sincere effort to restrict class discussion to the broad concerns that affect and have utility to all. Nothing pollutes a review effort as quickly as the occasional knucklehead who monopolizes the discussion and insists on chatting about his particular concerns at the expense of all others. This klutz should be referred to the teacher's office hours arrangements, where he may (or may not) have greater freedom to debate reality.

EXPOSURE TO PEER PERFORMANCE

As touched on earlier, performance classes provide students with ample opportunities to watch their peers perform. But in classes evaluated by forced-answer exams, it is not so simple.

With these classes, exam review provides almost the only opportunity for students to observe and learn from their colleagues' efforts. A history student, for example, may think she has a firm grasp on the causes of Tzar Svdllz's violent overthrow in the year 4, but until she listens to a classmate's exposition of the situation, she might remain unaware of the historical importance of flatulence suppression among royalty. It is unimportant whether the noisome problem hastened the Tzar's exit, but only that the student is exposed to her colleagues' ideas, insights, and techniques.

"Praise in public, condemn . . ." One aspect of peer performance that all students should be exposed to more than is common, is success. The topic doesn't really matter. Whether Alphonse has his Nobel Prize efforts commented on favorably, or that Kenny Slcnyz is applauded for finally demonstrating an ability to both spell and pronounce his last name, public commendation is indicated, appreciated by all hands, and surely worth the small class time cost.

TEACHER INTROSPECTION

A major function of postexam activities is to provide the teacher with feedback regarding how well his teaching efforts have worked. "How well did I get it across? How much of what I hoped the kids would learn did they apparently learn? How good was the exam?" Inspiration for these internal posttest discussions is generally triggered by two feedback sources: item analysis and student input.

With essay exams, item analysis efforts are too often encountered during the late-night marking festivities, or when the teacher enters individual grades into her gradebook:

- How is the class doing overall?
- How is each individual student doing?
- How come so many students missed question number 345?

But there are other, less publicized, teacher-appreciated functions. From time to time, review efforts provide the teacher (nobody we know, of course) with embarrassing but useful personal insights. One such flash of awareness might be called the "'Wow! Remind me never to ask that sort of idiotic question again!' syndrome." This occurs when it becomes clear that a particular question is a member of a large and tiresome group of questions that, for one of many reasons, should be avoided at all cost. Insultingly easy? Pointlessly difficult? Accidental but nevertheless unfortunate references to the superintendent's relatives? Whatever.

Another occurs (and is the basis for many teachers' nightmares) when in the process of explaining "the" answer, the teacher realizes in her heart of hearts that she doesn't know what she is talking about. This has been referred to as the "'Lordy! I've been teaching this nonsense as fact for my entire career! How come I never thought of . . .' syndrome."

ITEM ANALYSIS

Item analysis is the process of analyzing overall student response to individual test questions. This process generally has little immediate effect on the students, but it can be extremely useful to the teacher and next semester's students. A few minutes spent on item analysis both before and during review efforts may not do much to increase the relevance and validity of the current exam, but it can do wonders to improve on next year's instruction and exams. Classroom-adequate item analysis is so quick, easy, and useful that it should be more common. The sorts of information the teacher may find useful include items such as

- Questions that all students get right—or wrong—are useless. By failing to help separate the sheep from the goats, these questions have no validity.
- If only one student gets a particular question right (*or* wrong), it might be the most useful and discerning question on the exam.
- Questions that generally high-scoring students get wrong while generally low-scoring students get right, are bad questions—little validity.
- Blank answers. Why did so many otherwise rational students fail to respond to the question.

The item analysis process is particularly easy with some test-marking machines and almost any computer software programs intended for teacher use. Typically, the teacher enters the scores into the computer, tells the machine to item analyze the results and, in a matter of microseconds, out pops a report showing how many, and which, students missed which questions. Armed with this information, the teacher can approach the review period with much greater insight:

> Nobody got question seven right. How come? What's wrong with it?

All exam questions allow one more choice than appearances suggest: the unmarked answer. Pretest instructions and/or threats of great bodily harm notwithstanding, some students will leave some questions blank. What's a hardworking teacher to do? Simply marking the blank answer wrong is the obvious and typical response, but one that ignores some possibilities. For example, questions that most students leave blank and questions that only the better students generally leave blank are highly suspect; this situation should raise some questions in the teacher's mind:

- Is the student simply following the foolish instruction not to guess?
- Is the question not understood?
- Were there time constraints?
- What about lack of motivation?

Without microchip assistance, a complete item analysis probably takes more time and dedication than most teachers feel is justified, but if the students are made active participants in the effort during the review, a great deal of useful analysis can still be accomplished in the time appropriately available:

> Let's see the hands of those who got number seven correct. Nobody? Wow. What's wrong with it?

With machine-graded exams, one semi-heretical forced-answer technique that can inspire greater participation in the review process is to *refrain* from marking either the incorrect answers or the letter grade on the students' answer sheets. The kids get an answer sheet with only the number of correct answers shown—no indication of which answers are right or wrong, nor any indication of the letter grade. With only the raw score marked on the paper, virtually every student becomes utterly certain that he has been skewered—hideously mismarked ("I can't possibly have missed that many!"). He is far more likely to pay close attention to the exam's review until the last bitter pill is swallowed—that, of course, being the announcement of the letter grade ranking.

"But," you mutter, "what's to prevent a student from methodically changing any/all answers?" Surprisingly, this problem seldom comes up. With essay exams, it is virtually impossible for the sneaky student to change a grade-significant number of offending responses undetectably and in the time available. With machine-marked papers, mark changing is not virtually impossible, it *is* impossible. Even with pencil fill-ins, mark changing happens far less often than one might expect. However, if this becomes a problem, there are several possibilities:

- Simply refuse to change any scores. This is the easiest and simplest solution, and probably is as fair as most other parts of the evaluation process.
- Insist that the papers have no erasures, or that the exam be marked in ink. This is about as clever as asking somebody to do a crossword puzzle in ink.
- Photocopy selected papers prior to their return, and when the suspect student displays her "incorrectly marked" paper, present her (in private) with the copy made earlier. This generally brings this sort of fraud to a halt with admirable promptness. But as this hardnosed silliness is time consuming, it should be reserved for the rare student who may benefit from such foolishness.

ARBITRATION

Arbitration may be thought of as a personal review—usually one-on-one—and in private. It is particularly useful to the student who may still be perplexed or otherwise unhappy about the exam results and wants to discuss them. In the absence of formal arbitration-useful office hours, the teacher should at least make clear to the People Who Count that she is indeed available for one-on-one review efforts. And of course, arbitration can be particularly important to the occasional student who is hesitant to ask a question in front of the whole class lest he "look stupid."

DEFENSE

A seldom discussed but extraordinarily important function of testing efforts is the defense it can provide the teacher when the inevitable objections to her methods, judgments, and basic existence arise. When the parent storms into the conference room demanding to know, "How come my kid got a miserable little D in your miserable two-bit class?" simply stating, "In my opinion, that's what your kid earned," is not going to turn the scene into one of smiley faces. The teacher will be expected to back up her experienced and subjective estimate of student progress with a *written* experienced and subjective estimate of student progress. While this process is not notably productive, it happens, and without appropriate prior planning, the first hostile parent conference is likely to reduce the teacher to roadkill.

Unquestionably the most useful and effective grades-related defensive tool is candor—up front and ongoing. There will be far fewer problems down the road if the teacher assures that her grading philosophy, expectations, and procedures are clearly understood by the People Who Count. No matter the format—written exams, personal observation, or sheer tonnage of assignments turned in—her intentions should be made clear early in the semester and by all possible means—open house presentations, e-mails, letters home, or carrier pigeons.

Along with a clear start-of-term statement of intended grading procedures, it is important that the People Who Count are kept informed as the semester progresses. This suggests an "open gradebook" approach in which the teacher's gradebook (with adequate privacy provisions in place) is completely open at all times. Before the common availability of computers and adequate software programs, there was no convenient way for a class of thirty kids and their parents to have regular access to the information in the gradebook. But now it is so easy to calculate, print, and post complete gradebook information on a regular basis, weekly perhaps, that such should be common practice in all classrooms.

Consider the following scenario: Highly irate parents show up for a parent-teacher conference (generally far too late in the semester to accomplish much), demanding to know why neither they nor Sweet Alphonse were made aware of his shortcomings.

Parent, lovingly patting Alphonse's pointy head: I mean, like we can't help Alphonse learn no grammar unless you, like, keep us up to date.

Ms. Hardscrabble: Absolutely. That's why I've posted a computer printout of the complete gradebook every Monday since the start of the semester. Alphonse knew he had a D at the end of the first week, and until he turns in an occasional assignment, he is likely to remain, academically speaking, dead.

All eyes turn to Alphonse, who is last seen slowly sinking beneath the table.

A common defense-related practice, morally reprehensible and highly recommended, is to use official-looking gradebook entries to provide a fraudulent aura of mathematical precision to grading processes that are far from precise. PE, art, music, and other attitude/performance teachers are often stuck with a need to assign grades for such attributes as "sportsmanship," "appreciation of others' success," "teamwork," "musicianship," and other fuzzily defined attitudes and attributes which quite properly form the fundamental structure of quality programs. These teachers often spend hours struggling with irrelevant assessment procedures whose sole utility is to provide defensive gradebook numbers:

PE teacher to self: Lessee. Two points for clean sox, three for shoes that match, minus ten for snickering at Suzy's absurd performance . . .

This is not to suggest that the competent teacher can't accurately evaluate these characteristics; she certainly can, and when only the teacher and student are concerned, a personal discussion is completely adequate. But when others are involved, when the teacher's grades are challenged, numbers in the gradebook—no matter how irrelevant to actual evaluation—can be marvelously supportive. If the teacher can point to a neat column of computerized numbers in the gradebook, all will be well. Or at least better. Good enough.

But what if none of the above works? What if the parents remain obdurate and unconvinced? A defensive technique that works amazingly well is to simply give up. The parents arrive at the appointed hour, angry and demanding to know "What the hell is going on here?" (Actually with *that* sort of opening statement, the teacher is well advised to close her mouth, her gradebook, and her briefcase, and take a walk.) The teacher tries to explain, tries to be reasonable, but nothing works. What to do? Give up.

> Teacher: Okay, Mr. and Mrs. Sackbutt, you win. I'll give Sweet Alphonse any grade you want. Name it.
> Parent: You won't really change the grade.
> Teacher: Try me. An A costs me exactly as much as an F. What grade does Al deserve?
> Parent: (Pause) Well, actually . . .We weren't interested in the grade as *such*, but . . . er . . . um . . . Tell us. What did Sweet Alphonse actually *do*?

Right! Once the letter grade is eliminated as something to fight over, it is amazing how quickly the parents stop whimpering and get on with a useful discussion of Sweet Alphonse's academic progress—such as it may be. Not, one notes, exactly what Sweet Alphonse has in mind.

And then what does the teacher do when the exceedingly rare parents insist on a grade change? Same thing. She gives up. She changes the grade. She changes the permanent record to read, "Grade of D changed to A at parents' request," (giving Alphonse's next teacher a little advance warning), and takes a hike. She's done her best for the student, it hasn't worked, and she has better things to do than argue with cretins.

It is a temptation to say that it is the Sackbutt's problem now, but it isn't.

It's Sweet Alphonse's.

www.ingramcontent.com/pod-product-compliance
Lightning Source LLC
Chambersburg PA
CBHW020752230426
43665CB00009B/571